Sue Kenney's
My Camino

Sue Kenney's
My Camino

White Knight Publications
Toronto Canada

Published in 2004 by White Knight Publications,
a division of Bill Belfontaine Ltd.
Suite 103, One Benvenuto Place
Toronto Ontario Canada M4V 2L1
T. 416-925-6458 F. 416-925-4165 Toll-free 1-866-370-9407
e-mail <whitekn@istar.ca>

First Printing - June 2004
Second Printing - September 2004
Third Printing - October 2004

Order Information

Canada- Hushion House Publishing	USA - Hushion House Publishing
c/o Georgetown Terminal Warehouses	c/o Stackpole distribution
34 Armstrong Avenue	7253 Grayson Road
Georgetown, ON L7G 4R9	Harrisburg, PA 1711 USA
T. 1-866-485-5556 F. 1-866-485-6665	T. 1-888-408-0301 F. 1-717-564-8307
e-mail: orders@gwcanada.com	

National Library of Canada
Cataloguing in Publication
Kenney, Sue
Sue Kenney's my camino.
ISBN 0-9734186-3-X

1. Kenney, Sue—Journeys—Spain, Northern. 2. Spain,
Northern—Description and travel. 3. Christian pilgrims and pilgrimages
—Spain—Santiago de Compostela. 4. Santiago de Compostela (Spain)
I. Title. II. Title: My camino.

DP43.2.K44 2004   914.6'1   C2004-900382-8

Cover and text design: Karen Petherick, Intuitive Design International Ltd.
Font: Goudy
Editing: Bill Belfontaine, Bruce Pirrie
Photos: from the Author's collection.
Cover photo: Yanka & Yolanda Van der Kolk
Photo page 75: Emily Magee
Printed and Bound in Canada

The author has made every effort to contact the copyright holders
of material produced in this book. We would be pleased to have any additional
information regarding this material.

DEDICATION

To all pilgrims.

May you find peace and love on your journey,
wherever that might be.

ACKNOWLEDGEMENTS

My gratitude goes to all the pilgrims in the world over the past 1000 years who have kept the Camino alive with their step.

Each person in my life has added to the person I am. Special love and gratitude goes to my daughters, Tara, Meghan and Simone for their unconditional love and blessings on our life journeys. To John Kenney, my model of a great storyteller. To my mother, June Regan and my father, the late Bill Regan for your love and perpetual life lessons. Many thanks go to my siblings Patricia Harber, the late Donna Graham, Lorie Bos, Joanne Scott, Larry Regan, Kelly Gibbs and their beautiful families for their loving encouragement and support. To my lifetime friend Luba Paolucci, I am eternally grateful for your friendship and passion for my dream. With thanks to my friend Audrey Smith, whose creative talents and spiritual enlightenment have inspired me. Special thanks to my friends and collegues in the corporate world. I am sincerely thankful for the all incredible friends I have in my life.

To my rowing friends, crews and coaches especially Paul Westbury, Peter Cookson and the people at the Argonaut Rowing Club. To Marcia Martin for teaching me so many valuable life skills. Forever, I will be thankful to my pilgrim love, Andreas Laus especially for the miracle on Cebreiro. I am beholden to Bill Belfontaine for believing in my story from the very beginning. To Karen Petherick, book designer, for her intuitive creativity in bringing this book together. Special thanks goes to Bruce Pirrie for your gracious writing advice, editing and comic relief.

Special thanks to my friends and neighbors in and around Washago for their support.

I am eternally grateful to all the pilgrims on my path, the volunteers and especially the people of Spain for their part in showing me the way. I thank God.

A pilgrim always says thank you.

CONTENTS

INTRODUCTION

In the *Devil's Dictionary*, Ambrose Bierce defines a pilgrim as a traveler who is taken seriously. In other sources, a pilgrim is described as someone who embarks on a journey to a sacred spiritual place in search of a specific outcome. It is said that pilgrims have been chosen to walk without a clear understanding of why they are there, often guided by a higher source.

I am a pilgrim. I walked the Camino because I was lost in a society that valued material goals. My desire to be a pilgrim connected to a longing to belong somewhere in the world. To have peace and happiness with a knowing I was finally home through the discovery of self-love. By surrounding myself in a variety of natural settings, I dreamed of becoming a part of the grandeur of the universe.

The Camino Frances, is known because of the millions of pilgrims who have walked this 780 kilometer route that begins by crossing the Pyrenees mountains and then onto Santiago, Spain. This path has been traversed by people from around the world; their personal continuum of discovery. The name *Camino* itself translates to *the way* because its various routes all lead the way to the burial place of St. James the Apostle. I was optimistic that by walking the path alone in the winter it would be *the way* for me to face my deepest fears.

By living the simple life of a pilgrim – everyday just walking, eating, drinking, contemplating and sleeping – I would embark on a new life journey. This gave me the opportunity to finally be alone to walk into the shadows of the darkness and the healing light of my own true self. I was expecting to learn lessons on the Camino that would become a metaphor for my personal life journey. Simplicity and solitude would provide a perfect setting to distill them with the ultimate goal of defining my higher purpose.

People often asked if I was afraid to go on the Camino alone. Truly, I never questioned my fears about walking alone or whether I would make it to Santiago because I started this journey with an idea in my mind – I had already finished it. Several days before leaving for Spain it all became clear to me. There was an intuitive knowing that I had already been to Santiago, although I still had to go through the physical endurance of walking, to complete the passage to a more enlightened life.

Working on this book there were many days of fear. I was afraid I had undertaken this overwhelming task without the experience, formal education and talent of a seasoned writer. By facing fear on the Camino, I had learned the secret to creating my earnest desires. In the end, the creation of the book was not about having the skills of a writer, I could learn those; it was based on having clarity and vision about a message guided from a place of love.

I invite you to embrace the mystical pilgrim world of My Camino. As you journey through the stories, concentrate on being present with me. Calm your thoughts and allow your mind to open by letting go of all judgments and expectations. Then, surrender yourself to the possibility of being inspired in some way, as I take you on my journey.

Buen Camino.

HISTORY OF THE CAMINO
CAMINO DE SANTIAGO DE COMPOSTELA

Pilgrims have been traveling to Santiago de Compostela in Spain on foot, or by horseback (more recently by bicycle) for over eleven hundred years. One of the first pilgrims was Godescalc, the Bishop of Le Puy, who went there in 951 to venerate the supposed bones of St. James.

The Legend of St. James has it that after the death of Christ, his apostles were scattered to evangelize different parts of the world, as it was known then. St. James went to Spain where he did not meet with a great deal of success. He returned to Jerusalem with a few disciples and was beheaded by Herod Agrippa in 44AD. His followers rescued his remains and carried them down to sea where they miraculously embarked his body to the scene of their master's teaching. The truth of this is not possible to really say, but St. Aldhelm of Malmsbury knew St. James' preaching in 709 and news of the body being discovered had reached Lyon in France by 850.

According to an 11th century document, the burial place was revealed to a hermit Pelayo who told his bishop, Theodomir. He found the bodies of the apostle and his two disciples and built a church over their remains. The name of the place, Santiago de Compostela, refers to campus stellae, "the field of the star," reflecting the hermit's vision, perhaps or compostae, meaning "cemetery."

Santiago gained popularity in the Middle Ages when Jerusalem was held by the infidels and when the popes granted various and sundry indulgences in the 13th century for having made a pilgrimage. To the Church fathers, the venue was a worthy one because of the presence of an apostle's relics, it was far away and difficult to reach and it required a good deal of hardship and endurance to get there. There were wolves, unscrupulous people, bandits and a struggle with the non-believers. The rich, who sometimes went on the pilgrimages themselves, often hired pilgrims to walk the Camino for them and could buy indulgences. Criminals could serve their jail sentences by walking the Camino until their leg irons wore off or until they presented themselves at the Cathedral.

The Camino de Santiago is not one route, but in fact, many, extending throughout Europe toward a fixed point, Santiago de Compostela were the Saint's bones are still kept and venerated in a crypt beneath the Cathedral's main altar. The Codex Calixtinus, written for Pope Calixtinus in the 1300s was one of the very first travel guides, telling medieval pilgrims what to wear, how to pray and where to go, alerting them to possible dangers and miracles along the way.

Modern pilgrims each have their own way of making a pilgrimage and those ways are as myriad and as varied as the pilgrims themselves. There are the paths of the *faithful* – pilgrims that go to pilgrim's masses in each town, visiting various churches, monasteries and convents. For some, there is a special significance as pilgrims ponder their relationship to their faith and religious backgrounds and beliefs. There are the cultural spiritual, historical and physical paths pilgrims walk and perhaps a blending of each.

The landscapes of the Camino take on new dimensions as both inner and outer journeys.

Kathy Gower, Ph.D.

a modern day pilgrim

*O*ur bodies move in precision gracefully gliding as one force caressing the still water below, as if being led by the rhythm of a secret dance. My mind was calm. My soul surrendered in a balanced state without resistance as our crew of eight strong women rowed precisely in rhythm along the shores of Lake Ontario.

It is 5:00 a.m. Darkness blankets the vitality of the lake that rests on the shores of the still sleeping city of Toronto. Our coxswain, Ann, lies in the bow of the boat steering the course while calling out the training drill. Each of the rowers in our crew obediently aligns with stroke as she leads us to work in concert through a unified timing. The set cadence acts like a mantra that frees the mind to focus the core body on the application of power transferred and then released. At precisely the same time, each rower presses into the foot stops set in the belly of the boat. Our arms act as a leverage to the long oars gently cutting the blade into the moving water in anticipation of that precise moment of contact that will unify the crew's combined power to hurtle the boat forward.

The boat releases the sound of air bubbles beneath, a sign

it is running efficiently over the water. Suspended in movement, there is an ever-so-slight resistance felt as the oar collar makes contact with the back of the oarlock with a solid chunk. This is followed by a familiar whooshing sound as the crew presses through the water in unison. In a moment of transformation, the boat and crew's 1500 pounds propel forward with force and grace, followed by a pause as we recover in preparation for the next stroke.

Over the past six years I had taken up the sport of rowing, initially to overcome the despair I felt over my younger sister Donna's diagnosis of terminal cancer. By putting my anger into the water, I believed this allowed me to be more present to the needs of Donna, her three young boys, and less encumbered with my own sorrow. It helped me emotionally as I floundered in sadness to accept her last days on earth, only fifteen months later.

Unexpectedly, my fondness for the sport grew and soon I was training and competing as a master rower. In summer 2001, following 38 days of tryouts, I had made the crew selection for a priority boat destined to represent Canada at the 28th World FISA Master's Rowing Championships in Montreal, Quebec. I was to be rowing in the company of national level athletes like Maureen, who had rowed with Princeton's crew. Cathy and Jen had rowed in university, each one excelling in the sport to reach national level status. Gina had been rowing at a competitive level since high school. Kathy was our bow person and one of the novice rowers together with Cori and me, who had taken up rowing as a sport in mid-life.

The average age of our eight woman crew was 42 years! The youngest person was Erin, an unbelievable athlete at 34.

We competed in the A category against other boats with an average crew age of 27 to 34 years and in spite of our age, we won a gold medal. With the pride and glory of a world master's gold medal around my neck, I still longed for more in my life. Something was missing.

In October of 2001, I was a well-paid account executive with an international high-tech corporation working in Markham, Ontario. Often I worked at home or at the client's office in downtown Toronto. Earlier that week, the Vice-President of Sales had asked me to come to the office for a meeting on Monday morning at 9:00 a.m. Arriving early, I checked my voice mail, updated my greeting and then went to the meeting room to find the door closed. When I entered, I thought I recognized the woman from the Human Resources department sitting on the far side of the boardroom table looking rather stoic and holding a file folder in front of her. I tried to gather my composure as I became immediately more aware that one of my deepest fears was now a reality. I was about to face the process so very active in business practices today: corporate downsizing.

The Vice-President of Sales was standing directly behind me. He suggested I sit down and without delay I was informed that my position was redundant. I was handed a package and encouraged to read the material at a later time when I could better distill the situation. I was asked to turn in my corporate credit card, cell phone, personal organizer, laptop and company ID card. The woman took me to my desk, offering me a cardboard box for my personal belongings. Many of my colleagues stopped by to offer their genuine regrets and best wishes. Rummaging through my desk drawers in a state of embarrassed shock, it was obvious I was not yet fully aware of the implications of losing my job. Once I had gathered my personal things, I was escorted to the side doors of the building, and through them for the last time. This resulted in a blunt ending to my lifetime career in the corporate world of telecommunications. I felt so very much alone.

I was a single mother and world class rower, without a job. The entire telecom market had weakened and the prospects for another position in that industry were dim. My identity was wrapped around the roles of being a mother, athlete and a business woman. The abrupt changes to my secure roles had appeared suddenly leaving me feeling abandoned and hollow. Driving home, I found myself seriously considering what to do with my life. This was a perfect time for me to consider recreating myself.

After my marriage separation, our three children came to live with me in Toronto. John, their father, had moved about two hours east of the city to be in a small town, something he had always dreamed of doing. My oldest daughter Tara, who was 19 at the time, went to university at Kings College and was now living in London, Ontario. During the past summer, my youngest daughter Simone, who was 14 years old decided she would be going to live with her dad to start high school there. This was a new stage of her life and it was likely she would complete her education there. A feeling of grief overtook me as I imagined her not living with me for the next four years – and possibly longer.

Meghan, my middle daughter was 16. She would be finishing high school in June of that year with plans to go to university or college. It was likely she too would be moving out. My nurturing role was changing whether I liked it or not.

Soon the house would be empty. As teenagers, many of their life lessons are learned through experience not by what I could teach them. This forced me to let go of my desire to keep control over their lives.

As their independence strengthened, my motherly efforts evolved to the role of a guide. I could show my daughters the way, but I could not take them there. There was a degree of satisfaction in guiding their souls that ultimately revealed my maternal desire to nurture other souls in the universe, in the same way. This was a turning point for me as I began a new search for my feminine role – one that didn't involve climbing the corporate ladder to success.

It was mid-morning when I finally arrived home. I hoped my friend and next door neighbor, Lucy, would be there to offer some sensible advice, but her driveway was empty. I left my little box of personal belongings on the floor inside the door. The house was quiet. Walking into the kitchen, I sat at the table not really sure about what to do next. My eyes wandered over the material things I had acquired, realizing how little they meant to me anymore. I felt sad and depleted of life's passion. There must be something I could do, I thought, to bring more meaning to my existence.

And so the journey begins ...

prelude to a journey

*A*s a child, I remember the feeling that I was special in a particular way. Unable to define what was different about me, I just remember feeling out of place almost constantly. My sisters and brother always referred to me as the black sheep of the family. I was independent, rebellious, unafraid of the unknown, and I would try anything once. At first I resented their description, but eventually accepted myself, preferring to extend my comfort zone, to challenge myself, and experience all the things that were possible in life. I was definitely not prepared to settle for mediocrity.

Growing up in Toronto, I became aware of how people expressed love for themselves. My parents only had enough money to get by from week to week. This meant I couldn't have many of the things I yearned for until I was old enough to get a job and buy them myself. Among new friendships, especially those whose priorities were money and material possessions, I observed that they seemed to be happier. Is it possible they knew how to love themselves? It made sense to me that I should use these same values to develop well-adjusted, socially acceptable children. Didn't every parent want the best schools, the best music and dance lessons, the best sports coaches and more for their children? My children were raised in a Catholic home with strong Christian values. Regardless, I felt the material world was a continually over-riding factor.

I was raised a Catholic and I believed that God loved everyone unconditionally. If I did something bad, I could confess and seek reconciliation, knowing that God would still love me. For this, I loved God. In return God gave love and I gave love back. Simple as it was, I craved to discover more about universal love.

In my childhood years, my dad was never home. My mother was often left with all seven children to care for alone. She attempted to share her love with each of us equally often commenting she had none left at the end of the day. My interpretation of this was that she did not have any love left to give to herself after we had demanded most of it from her. I wanted so much to help. Being the second oldest child it became my intention to give my younger siblings all my love so that my mother would have some love left for herself. In my adult life, just like my mother, I ran out of love too.

My father was an alcoholic. He passed away a few years ago after a long battle suffering with complications from diabetes. All of my life, I strove to make him proud of me in everything I did. As an adult child of an alcoholic parent, it was typical to want to please everyone, except myself.

Throughout my teenage years, the woman's code that could become my destiny began to unfold. I learned to reward myself in an attempt to mirror self-worth by treating myself to something special, like buying a new pair of shoes or spending a day at the spa. This, I assured myself, was self-love. By rewarding myself in this manner, I was fulfilling the immediate needs of my ego, leaving my soul to wither away. I was unable to resist the social pressures of an urban materialistic environment that was all around me.

During my lifetime I was conditioned and socialized to believe that I would marry, have a family, a career, a dog, two cars, a house and a cottage. As expected, I fell in love, married my high school sweetheart and we had three beautiful daughters. I love being a mother and teaching my children about life values preparing them for their own journey as a contribution to the world. Everything looked perfect on the outside to everyone else, except for me, there was a certain emptiness associated with the attainment of material things and money.

While working at Bell Canada, I had a career, making decent wages with all the benefits. I "drank the kool-aid" of the corporate world, climbing the ladder to reach my dreams and aspirations to become a successful businesswoman. Soon, I was making a six figure income while working in the UK as an international consultant.

My desire for self-love became secondary while we maintained a goal-oriented lifestyle as a family. My life grew more complicated and busy. Each moment accounted for and every detail planned with the intent of reaching a goal for greater success. This was not my nature but 20 years with Bell Canada had molded me into a task-oriented individual. I truly desired more creativity in my life, but I felt that now was not the right time for me, so I waited.

Working in a corporate culture, my spiritual self felt deserted and longed for more attention. Soon, I was reading everything I could find about universal love, awareness and alternative approaches to an enlightened way of living. I discovered Sufism, Druidism, Buddhism and whatever I could find to give me a new perspective to living a more spiritual life. It appeared the theme of awareness, love, truth, surrender, serving and mystical marriage was present everywhere I looked.

Truly believing I could accomplish anything I desired, my ongoing frustration was imbedded in the inability to grasp and commit to what it was I truly desired. Convinced that once I was clear about my true desires, then I would accept full accountability to make them a reality.

Several years ago while I was working and living in England, I had a unique opportunity to do a parachute jump. I was nervous and yet completely open to the opportunity to face my fear of heights. That day, we spent eight hours as a group learning about safety and technique. We practiced different approaches to landing on the ground. I will never forget the words of the instructor just before we boarded the small plane. He told us not to think about all the things we learned that day. He said, "Forget everything except these three things; when you land on the ground, keep your feet together or you will break your legs; don't point your toes downward because when you land you will break both your feet; whatever you do, do not land on pavement." He paused for emphasis. "I don't want to tell you what will happen then." He was the expert and I trusted his advice but I wondered about the purpose of spending eight hours learning skills we were supposed to forget.

As we took off, we sat in deadly silence, each of us coming face to face with our innermost fears. I was the last person to jump and I had watched everyone else in their moment of truth. Sitting on the floor of the plane, with my legs dangling high in the air, I started to pray promising that if I lived I would be a more loving person and serve others.

I jumped. The silence of the fall was glorious. There was a virgin-like atmosphere at that height where I felt a complete connection with the universe as I floated gracefully downward. About 500 feet above the ground the liberating freedom of gently falling abruptly turned into panic. The ground appeared to be rushing up to me at a speed I couldn't control. I was going to die! Trying to gain some composure I suddenly remembered our instructor had warned us about this feeling he called "ground rush." Although I'd moved closer to the earth, nothing else had changed except my perspective of where the ground was in relation to the speed of my fall. Moving closer to the ground, it became more obvious that I would be fine if I just landed with my feet and legs together. I touched down in a corn field jolting my entire body with the force of the fall. I waited wondering if anything had broken but I was perfectly fine. As I gathered the parachute, I promised myself that I would consciously begin the process of facing my deepest fears, in whatever form they took.

When we married, John and I had worked hard renovating our home. We made a number of good real estate decisions giving us the privilege of acquiring a house, a cottage and all the conveniences that come with that type of lifestyle. We aligned completely with the social structure of the great American Dream only to find in the end, John was content, but I wasn't. I had achieved my material goals but I had found almost no spiritual fulfillment.

I hated that nagging little voice in my mind, a driving

force telling me not to give up on my search. When we were married, John would often question why I wasn't grateful for what I had accomplished. He couldn't understand why I was always searching for more, thinking my search was for success in the material world. On the other hand, I didn't understand how John could be so content to accept everything the way it was. I thought he didn't have ambition, but maybe I was wrong. Maybe he had already been on the inner journey that I longed to experience.

Frustrated with this ongoing internal battle, I thought there was something wrong with me. Many of my friends were reaching middle age, slowing down their lifestyles, beginning to give up on life dreams they hadn't yet achieved. I decided I was not giving up that easily. Certain that there wasn't another option, with painstaking consideration, I faced one of a woman's deepest fears and ended a marriage of 20 years with a wonderful man. Like the parachute jump I took the plunge and leapt into the world for a second time, this time without a parachute.

Years later, I was at home watching TV in the early evening. I was always doing two or three things at the same time, so it was usual for me to channel hop. I found many of the programs intriguing but they could not hold my attention for very long. Flipping around, I stopped at a travel show profiling walking tours in Spain. The clip showed a short piece about a pilgrimage route called the Camino de Santiago. I watched with interest, although I never considered the idea of actually doing the walk. It required at least a month to complete and my life at that time was complicated as a single working mom with a rented house and three teenage daughters living with me. To top it off, I was also rowing six days a week. There was no time in my life left to go for a walk. A few months later, while channel hopping I again turned to the same travel documentary. This time I was drawn to watch with deepened interest. The Camino had presented itself to me again and I realized there was a message for me on that 19 inch screen. Was it for me alone?

Later that day I wrote the word Camino on a sticky note and left it on the kitchen table. A few days passed and I did an Internet search on the word Camino. What I found was overwhelming. The history of the ancient pilgrimage route was revealed through stories of the people of Spain, as past and modern-day pilgrimage accounts and journals, as well as written tales of folklore and miracles. I could relate to the stories of the pilgrims who embarked on a spiritual journey because they were just like me. I was intrigued by the prospect of walking outdoors for a month, without modern conveniences, following yellow arrows on a path that led pilgrims on a journey into unknown territories, both physical and spiritual. From what I had read about the mystical nature of pilgrimages, I knew if the Camino was right for me it would find a way to fit itself into my busy life. I just did not know how it would.

My philosophy about life had evolved and I believed that to achieve true happiness, every thought, action, emotion, and intention should come from a place of love; as love is the essence of the soul. As my soul traveled on its life journey, a new message about love was presented. Many times in my life I had been told that before you can love someone else, you must love yourself first. That prompted me to consider many questions affirming my doubts about this statement being true.

It was unimaginable for me to act selfishly by assuming love for myself, before giving to others. Surely this was not suggesting that I should love myself before I loved God. I was confused.

It was obvious that to be congruent to living my life purpose from a place of love, I would first have to love myself. To find self-love, I must be completely accepting, without judgment. The concept of self-love was foreign to me seemingly misplaced in a society that worshipped material values and external goals. I decided to deviate from my present life and walk a pilgrimage. Embarking on this journey, I would travel alone in search of my sanctuary to experience what I affectionately came to refer to as, "having a love affair with myself."

daily meditations

alsa music, spicy food and excited conversation set the atmosphere at Hernando's Hideaway on Wellington Street in Toronto. It was November 4, 2001, the last day of a year-long self-development program led by a very dynamic woman, Marcia Martin. We were attending our graduation party. We had learned new life lessons to nourish possibilities in order to create the future we desired. Although we knew we always had the support of each other, now was the time we would venture alone to start another life odyssey armed with new insights.

The next morning, I would be on a flight to Paris to begin my journey of a solitary pilgrimage. My daughters, family and friends were genuinely concerned for my safety since no one had ever heard of something called the Camino, unless of course there was one parked in their driveway. It wasn't unusual for people who knew me to assume that I could get myself safely out of just about any situation. This time, however, even I wasn't so sure I could pull it off. I had researched the Camino only enough to expose the details I absolutely needed to know. I believed that too much information would have a negative impact on the mystery and excitement that comes with stepping into the unknown.

Back at Hernando's, there were hugs, kisses and tears as we said farewell to each other. While making my way around the room, I noticed Donna, my fellow workshop friend watching me. I had felt a special connection to her since she had the same name as my younger sister who had died of cancer. Her calm, composed manner seemed out of character, in the noisy action-packed bar. She grinned with a wide knowing smile, as she watched me work my way around the room. It was as though she had an understanding about me like she was privy to an intuitive insight to my deepest emotions and fears. She confidently waited, resting in what seemed like an aura of peace. As I got closer to her, I could feel my world slowing down in the presence of her calmness. She waited patiently for me to greet her.

Donna spoke slowly, carefully selecting every word. "Sue, you will be accompanied on your journey with a special gift from me. I am sending you some angels, to guide and protect you." Nodding my head I thanked her, holding back the urge to tell her I didn't actually believe she could send angels with me. In fact, I didn't even believe in angels, period. Donna was so sincere with her offer, I bit my tongue and thanked her, agreeing to accept the gift. Then she said, "Sue, I am sending 2000 angels with you."

This time I laughed out loud thinking she must be crazy. "Do you know 2000 angels, Donna?" I asked.

"Yes, I do," she said in a confident self-assured manner. I didn't know what more to say so I thanked her, gave her another hug, and walked away. Eventually, her generosity left my mind as I became totally absorbed in hurrying to say goodbye to the others. I had to get home to finish packing to leave the next day. I left feeling the familiar comfort of this special group of people, needing to embark on a whole new journey alone. I would completely forget about Donna's gift of 2000 angels, that is, until I saw them only two weeks later.

While packing that night, I started to seriously consider my reasons for taking this journey. In ancient times a pilgrimage was practised as a form of meditation, reconciliation, prayer or to help with healing. It was apparent to me that this modern day journey could conceivably address each one of these areas in my life and now I was ready to take the first step. My reasons for walking were precipitated by having available time and a desire to be alone, and a longing to understand my purpose in the universe.

On this pilgrimage, I wanted to journey to the most sacred place of all, to my soul. This was something that I'd longed for all my life. I wanted to go to a place where I could see the truth. Truth being absolute love shining in the face of the authentic self. The best way I thought this could be achieved was to establish a relationship with Mother Earth, the stars, planets, trees and the universe itself. To accomplish this I would spend time outdoors, living in the elements of the universe as a simple pilgrim, deliberately putting myself in a place outside the familiarity of my everyday life.

Like most people, I resist change by falling back on my old patterns of behavior. Knowing this led me to consider the idea of ritual and ceremony as part of my daily meditation. I read Gabriel Garcia Marquez's book, *Clandestine in Chile*, about the adventures of Miguel Littin a famous film director exiled from

Chile who returns to shoot a film. In preparation for entering the country, he changes his physical appearance, dress, speech, body and hand actions. He transforms himself from a casually dressed, bearded director to a Uruguayan businessman and describes the mental process of changing his identity as a daily battle. In the book he confirms that it wasn't learning a new behavior that was difficult for him, the challenge was in the body and mind constantly resisting the change.

On my life journey my body and mind resisted change too. Although, this time I didn't want to recreate my identity, I just wanted to become more of my own true self. Becoming a pilgrim presented an opportunity to peel away the layers that had been protecting me from the truth. It would involve a change in my behavior, dress, thoughts, and intentions. A shift to a simple life that would ultimately upset the established patterns of daily living. My pilgrim character was being created.

There was no suitcase with wheels for this trip, only a red backpack that would carry 25 pounds – all my worldly belongings. The sleeping bag was stuffed in the bottom. No pillow. Since I would be a transient, my sleeping bag represented my personal space. I would become very protective of what would be my only sense of a home for the next month. I wondered if this was the same fervor that homeless people living on the streets around the world feel in safeguarding personal things and space while in public places.

The tools I took included a utility knife and a first aid kit. No razors, tweezers, eyelash curlers or nail files. No make-up or deodorant. I included one of those sports towels that absorbs water off your body like a chamois. I took one pair of good leather hiking boots and track shoes thereby eliminating the need to make the ultimate female decision, what shoes to wear. I had two pairs of baggy hiking pants and two long-sleeved micro-fiber shirts, a jacket, fleece vest and jacket, rain pants, three pairs of socks and two pairs of sock liners. There were no push-up bras or silky thongs; I wasn't going on the Camino to impress anyone. I did take three identical pairs of plain black sport underwear that were comfortable, dried quickly and with panty liners, doubled as pajama bottoms. I wore a micro-fiber vest as a pajama top and as a first layer, under my clothes in the day. A pair of leggings would be a blessing on the cold days and nights ahead. Each item contributed to the costume of my new pilgrim persona.

Fortunately, the discipline of keeping a journal was already established from my rowing training. I planned to list my goals on the front page of my diary and made a commitment to read them each day. I wanted to develop a way of expanding the discipline for training my body in a sport, to create a more spiritual approach to training my subjective mind and to channel the direction of my intended energy. I did this by establishing rituals; a series of actions completed daily as a form of ceremony.

On the top of each page in my diary, I would note the date, destination, temperature and number of kilometers logged each day, to set the context of that day's experiences. My spiritual journey would involve both physical and emotional experiences, so I decided it was important for me to write the stories related to my mind, body and spirit happenings. Then I could write about the landscape, other pilgrims, the villagers and any other thoughts that were important to me. I would make a conscious effort to write directly from my heart with the intention of refraining from judging myself. By undertaking the ritual of journalizing, I hoped to discover a new state of awareness, to allow for an expression of my observations, from a brand new perspective.

Intentions use the power of the subjective mind to deliver that which is truly desired in the objective mind, by providing an active focus or commitment. I knew it was important to be specific and to only consider my most earnest desires; a wish is not strong enough. By using action words to create a sense of completion, I would actively be what I intended. By doing this I would be assured of the potential to manifest my desire.

> I am my higher purpose.
> I am self-love.
> I walk in a state of intent.
> I am present and aware.
> I have an open mind and an open body.
> I am creating my future.
> I am in a state of gratitude.
> My mind is clear in meditation.
> I learn something new every day.
> I notice my mood.
> I live my commitments.

As my goal for this journey was the discovery of my higher purpose, I would have to learn the secrets to mastering what I wanted to accomplish through ritual. I decided that each day I would spend the first hour walking in a state of increased presence and awareness. Concentrating on my breathing, I used a form of walking meditation to clear my thoughts. I imagined breathing in all the love of the universe as a white light, I would pause, holding the light within me as it illuminated my body and soul, then I would breathe my love out to the universe.

Self-love is both an emotion and a state of being. I would have to learn to recognize this emotion before I could begin to embody it. I could easily understand and strangely enough see the emotion of anger, but the emotion of self-love had to be re-defined for me. I thought about what a sensory state might look like. Questions arose; Would I be able to see self-love? What would it feel like? Could I touch it? Could I smell it? What would I hear? How would I know when I was there? How would I act? Again, in a state of awareness, I practised what it would be like to love myself, hoping the time could come when I would be able to feel self-love. Once I could feel it, I was assured of the possibility I would recognize it.

In my search for truth in life, I had studied different philosophies. The Dalai Lama talks about a great source of inspiration from the teachings of lo-jong, which means "transforming the mind to create happiness." I believed that to live from a place of truth, brings peace. Peace brings happiness. In a state of happiness I could be love and in a state of love, I could create more happiness.

I learned to approach each life experience as if it were presented on a flat plane in front of me. Positive experiences were seen on the plane to the right side and negative experiences were seen on the left. This contrasted with the habit of seeing good/positive things as "up" and bad/negative things as "down." Approaching things this way enabled me to level out my emotional reactions to different situations, whether they were positive or negative, ultimately reducing a lot of stress.

This reminded me of the experience I had during the rowing season in 2001. We were well into the crew selection process and now it was time to test our speed on the water by doing seat racing. This is a method of calculating the speed of each rower based on results achieved in multiple races with different partners in a pair; to my estimation one of the toughest boats to row since you have only two rowers, each one with an oar on either side of the boat. It's easy to flip, hard to steer and impossible to hide your shortcomings.

It was the day before the seat racing and I was already thinking of a dozen reasons why I wouldn't make the crew. I was too short, I didn't have a determined mind, and I hadn't been rowing as long as some of the others. The excuses went on and on. The only bright spot was that the coach had said I had arms like an ape, an advantage in this sport. I was afraid of my potential of being selected for a crew that actually went to the world championships with the chance of winning a gold medal. If anyone asked, I was going to give it my best shot. I knew I was in trouble at a friend's house when I asked him to help me get motivated. I had lost my edge. I had lost the fuel for my engine, my commitment.

We seat raced again and I blew almost every race. Rowing requires the delicate grace of a ballerina and the brute strength of a lumberjack equally combined. There was no grace or strength in the way I rowed that morning. My body was tense and controlled. The next day, our rowing coach, Paul Westbury, sent the results via e-mail. Each of the rowers were sorted into

A and B teams. The A group had won their seat in the final crew selection, but I was in the B group and I would have to be tested again to secure a seat. That night I decided I wanted to be a part of this crew.

Early the next morning, I raced again with renewed commitment and focus. Once the results were tabulated, Paul approached me to say I had made the crew. I jumped in excitement telling Paul not to worry I would not let him down. He said, "Don't do this for me, Sue. Do it for yourself."

Being in a crew boat is a place to practice life lessons to be learned in preparation for the real world back home. I felt comfortable learning from my mistakes on the Camino, but to face my fear I would have to completely surrender. My past interpretation of surrender meant I would have to concede, raise the white flag and give up having failed. This time it would be different. Fear had held me in place and now fear was letting me go.

4

early lessons

rior to Christopher Columbus discovering that the world wasn't flat, many pilgrims of the past followed the Camino path under the stars of the Milky Way and on to Fisterra. Fisterra actually means "the end of the earth." It was this place, on the most westerly part of the coast of Spain that the medieval pilgrims believed was the end of the world. For most pilgrims, the final destination is Santiago but a hardy few go onto Fisterra. Although I planned to walk to Santiago, I sensed that my spiritual destination would be enroute, on the mountain of Cebreiro. This was because while doing research on the Camino, I read about a miracle that took place there and right away, I felt that something euphoric was awaiting for me on that mountain, too.

In the early evening of November 5, 2001 I boarded a plane in Toronto, destined to arrive in Paris the next morning. From there, I would take a train to St. Jean Pied de Port, France. In the air, my entire being became anxious and deathly afraid of the unknown journey in store for me. My mind raced, imagining fear-inducing scenarios; language difficulties, getting lost, potential injuries, falling off a mountain, wild dog attacks, being robbed, beaten or worst of all, totally and utterly confronting my own shortcomings while being alone. If I really wanted to reach my goal, I knew I would have to face these fears walking the Camino, a place decidedly outside my comfort zone.

After eight hours in the air, I arrived in Paris, picked up my heavy backpack, and boarded a bus to the train station arriving with 15 minutes to spare. Using high school French, I somehow managed to obtain a train ticket to Bayonne, where I would change trains to go to St. Jean Pied de Port. While traveling on the train, my perspective was beginning to shift as I unconsciously took on the character of being a pilgrim. I couldn't see any other pilgrims on the train, but I found myself looking at my fellow travelers around me with a compassion for strangers I had never before experienced.

Eight hours out of Paris, the train pulled into the station in St. Jean Pied de Port at 8:40 p.m., exactly on time. Swinging my backpack over my shoulders, I stepped off the train onto the platform and headed towards the exit, with no idea where I was going. A friendly-looking man stood at the door and I asked in English if he knew where the pilgrim hostel was located. He gave me directions in French, pointing the way down the street. I listened carefully, but the inadequacies of my French language skills were confirmed and I became lost. I could not find the hostel anywhere. Roaming the streets in the dark with an uncomfortable heavy backpack was frustrating me. By 9:30 p.m., tired and hungry, I finally came upon a small hotel. For 240 French francs, I checked in and took a rattling one-person elevator to the fourth floor. There I found a little room with space for only a single bed and dresser. A huge double window with typical French shutters opened to the main street below. Checking the washroom facilities, I found a shower and a bidet. The toilet was down the hall, in the water closet.

I sat on the bed's soft mattress and dropped my cumbersome backpack onto the floor, wondering how I could carry such a heavy load across the Pyrenees mountains. I had read that 25 lb. or 11 kg was the optimum weight an average person could carry. Yet here I was, a trained athlete struggling with the weight I was carrying. It was time to shed some of the baggage I brought with me. I began by sorting through my belongings deciding what I could conceivably leave behind.

First, I considered the two books I brought on the history and art of the Camino, highly recommended on an Internet list service for pilgrims. I thought that I would have a lot of time to read in the evenings. Backpack lesson number one: books are very heavy to carry. I justified leaving the books behind by rationalizing I should spend time writing in my journal.

Backpack lesson number two: dispose of any excess clothing. With five different tops in my bag, I folded two long sleeve cotton T-shirts and placed them on the dresser for the chambermaids. I brought flip-flops for the shower, but they could go. The folding umbrella was not needed since I had a high-tech jacket to protect me from the rain. Looking over my hygiene products, I left a bar of soap, my face cream and emptied half the shampoo out of the bottle. I squeezed half the toothpaste out of the tube, hoping this would help in some small way, to reduce the weight. At home, it's expected to have more than you could ever possibly use and on the Camino I did. The cleaning staff must have a host of stories about the things pilgrims leave behind before embarking on their journey.

Regardless of what I had planned in Toronto, it was obvious my Camino was already unfolding in a direction that was decidedly out of my control. I could define my expectations for this walk and try to force them into being or I could surrender to the Camino. Paul Westbury, my rowing coach used to say, "The problem with rowers, is they slow the boat down." Rowing requires incredible, lasting strength and the ability to mentally and physically surrender to the fluidity of the boat permitting the equipment to do what it has been engineered to do, move through the water fast. I knew what he meant. The value of surrender was perfectly clear to me.

The very first time I rowed in front of our coach, Paul was in a boat following our crew of eight women from the Argonaut Rowing Club along the shores of Lake Ontario. Three kilometers later we reached the end of the course at the Humber River without having heard any coaching from him at all. This was most unusual since the role of a coach was to constantly point out what could be improved with an individual's stroke technique and the efficiency of the boat as a whole. This was generally done with ongoing communication from the coach in the form of yelling into a megaphone, to make sure he was heard.

While we rowed, I was intense and focused on my technique trying to achieve technical perfection in the areas of balance, power application and timing. When I first started rowing I was told that the perfect stroke had never been rowed. With about 250 individual movements in each stroke, I was determined to perform the perfect stroke and at the same time make a good first impression on the coach, who would be selecting the crew going to the world master's regatta. The intense concentration and focus left me physically exhausted and mentally drained by the time we reached the end of the course.

"Whyte, whyte, whyte. Staap, staap, staap!" Paul suddenly called to the coxswain in his thick New Zealand accent. We had trouble understanding him, and had never heard this command before in any language. Normally, the command used to stop the boat is "let it run," but we were to find out that Paul wasn't a normal coach. He was incredibly unique in communicating his style, technique, and personality. The boat eventually stopped and we all waited anxiously, breathing deeply in anticipation of his comments on the row. He maneuvered the coach boat toward us. I was horrified to see he was approaching me. The closer he got, the more worried I became. I had put everything I had into that three-kilometer row and if that was not good enough, then I would have to reconsider the possibility of reaching my dream to go to the world championships. I was giving up on myself even before I knew what he was going to say. Pointing the bow of the coach boat directly at me, he leaned forward. I sat taller. "Sue Kenney, will you please staap trying so hard?" I thought maybe I didn't hear him correctly because of his accent.

Surprised by this comment I said, "What do you mean staap trying so hard? That's what I do. I always try my best by putting 150% into every workout."

Again he said, "Well don't. You have the longest arms in the crew and you obviously know how to row, so would you please just row."

Confused, I slouched forward. I respected this man's

coaching ability and although I did not understand why he was discouraging me from trying my hardest, I decided to keep an open mind. Over the last five winters I had trained at the Canada Rowing Camp in Elberton, Georgia, and completed the second level of the coaching certification. Besides, I had learned a great deal about effective rowing technique, working with some of the best national level coaches in Canada and I still had not effectively combined the technical skills required. Maybe his approach would help me to do this.

We turned the boat around and started back towards the Argonaut Rowing Club. Resisting the desire to try hard was a new discipline for me. Instead, I just rowed along following the rhythm of the entire boat allowing the technical skills to find a place in the stroke. This opened a new experience, a profound sense of alignment combining my style with the graceful movement of the other rowers. My senses, awakened by the rush of water slithering under the shell, were producing goose bumps on my arms.

By not focusing on perfection that day, I rowed liberated. The return trip to the clubhouse was the ultimate rowing experience for me. Rowing without resisting the natural flow of the boat actually accomplished more with less effort, providing a level of joy and satisfaction I didn't know was possible. This method of coaching gave me confidence that the distillation of years of practise and study in the technical aspects of the stroke, could finally be released. All the energy I had expended on trying so hard for perfection had now become available to me. Paul taught me the importance of learning and practising technical aspects to create an efficient style by being a rower. In life, he gave me permission to just be Sue Kenney.

In my little hotel room in France, I listened to the activity on the streets outside, as I lay on the tiny single bed. On the edge of falling asleep, I thought about how much I wanted to be a pilgrim. My mind and body were alive with anticipation about learning the aspects of pilgrim life. That night, I began the process of surrendering to the Camino, fully aware that my body's strength and mental determination would take me across the north of Spain, on a spiritual journey to my soul.

Looking up at the cracks in the ceiling I thought about my studies in various philosophies, alternate wellness, yoga and meditation. For years I had been practicing different approaches to finding peace of mind and balance in my life. On the Camino, I would take the time to distill the knowledge I had acquired in my lifetime. I wanted to create a vision that would define the depth of my wisdom, so I could manifest it in my life. Wisdom, I surmised would become the conduit for the delivery of my life purpose. I had read that philosophy was defined as *a mystical woman whose soul is knowledge and her body is wisdom.* She was someone I wanted to be.

The Camino was designed to take pilgrims on a journey and I had already decided I was not going to make it any more difficult by adding resistance. I would surrender to what I knew I didn't have any control over. My eyes were getting heavy as I said a short silent prayer of thanks and set my watch alarm for 6:00 a.m. so I could begin walking bright and early. The droning noise outside became distant and I fell into a deep, peaceful sleep.

The next thing I heard was the sound of rain. Squinting to adjust my eyes to the daylight, I could not believe the time. It was 9:30 a.m.! I had slept in on my first day. I thought, this couldn't be happening. For many years I had been waking up before five o'clock in the morning to row. Encumbered with jet lag, the six-hour time difference and sixteen hours of travel in the last 24 hours had taken its toll on my plans for that day.

It was too late to start out now because I didn't have enough daylight; the sun would be down by six o'clock. The early part of my journey would require that I walk over the Pyrenees mountains from France to Spain, covering 27 kilometers to reach an altitude of 1500 meters, almost 5000 feet. This section alone could take up to 10 hours, my guidebook warned. Disappointed, I thought about the advice shared on the internet list services I had joined just before leaving; there was a taxi service available to Roncesvalles. It was perfect, I thought. Leaving my backpack in the hotel room, I set out for the Pilgrim's Office, where I would register as a pilgrim, obtain my credential and ask about the taxi. The credential, or official pilgrim passport, would permit me to have access to the hostels, known as refugios or albergues, situated in the villages, towns, and cities along the Camino.

The chill mountain rain fell all day leaving the cobblestone streets slick and slippery. Along the way, I discovered a lovely little patisserie where I bought French pastries, bread and Brie cheese for lunch. At a quaint gift shop, my search for a diary produced a perfect little red book with graph pages. I bought a few postcards and a phone card. Next stop was the Pilgrim's Office.

Following Rue de la Citadelle, I easily found the Pilgrim's Office for the Association les Amis du Chemin de Saint-Jacques (Association for the Friends of Saint James). Apprehensively, I peeked through the window to see a room filled with scores of maps and books all about the Camino. At a big desk, off to the right there was a friendly looking man sitting behind it busily doing paperwork. My heart raced as I entered this historic, typically elegant French-styled building. Facing two slender wood doors, I slowly turned the hefty door knob on the right and it swung open. I walked into the room, heavy with trepidation knowing that once I had my credential, I would be written into the history of the Camino and then I could not turn back. I was both wary and excited. I'm sure it showed in my flushed features.

A pleasant person greeted me in French as I smiled nervously, "Bonjour, je suis Sue Kenney, Canadian peregrina." Vous parlez Anglais?"

He said, "Yes, welcome, my name is Jacques."

I had been holding my breath since walking into the room and now, finally, I could breathe out. Strolling over to the front of the desk I stood there smiling at Jacques who was preparing to register me as a pilgrim. He filled out a standard form, beginning the process by asking general information about me. Then he requested to see my passport and noted the number. When he asked for my profession, I froze, realizing I did not have a job. Then, smiling in relief, I told him to just note my profession as *entrepreneur*, since I no longer identified myself with a corporate career.

Then for official purposes, Jacques asked me to declare my reason for walking the pilgrimage. He offered me four options: religious, spiritual, historical or other. "Spiritual," I said. He made a show of deliberately marking the appropriate box. Jacques then signed and handed me the credential. I was inducted into the history of the Camino as pilgrim number

5948, in the year 2001. This moment marked the beginning of an event that would change my life forever.

I explained to Jacques that I had slept in and I wanted to inquire about taking a taxi to Roncesvalles. His tone became very serious as he spoke about the dangerous weather possible on the Pyrenees. With the drama of an actor his outstretched arms waved as he spoke, "You are a strong woman, you should walk over the Pyrenees. Don't be afraid." I thought if he knows the dangers of the mountains and still believes I can do it alone, I should have faith in my ability trusting the Camino will take care of me. My commitment was again confirmed and unshakable. I would not take a taxi. I would walk up the mountain alone.

I asked Jacques if anyone had started the walk that day and he told me there was group of seven pilgrims who left yesterday morning, but I was to be the only one to walk the Pyrenees that day. Jacques gave directions to a Basques albergue in Hontos, about six kilometers uphill to the only village on the mountain. He kindly called ahead to book a room, which was not really necessary since I was the only pilgrim. We smiled, shook hands and I thanked him again for his help. As I turned to walk away, he called out. "You are a courageous woman. Buen Camino," he added with pride.

Having completed the first of many pilgrim rites and filled with a sense of belonging I walked through the slender doors onto the cobblestone street in a dreamlike state. I had become a pilgrim on the road to Santiago. While walking back leisurely to my hotel room, my imagination was unraveling romantic notions about a medieval voyage under the heavens, when the words of another rowing coach, Peter Cookson, came into mind. With a great deal of patience, Peter taught me how to row a single scull. To give me a different perspective about slowing down the mechanics of my stoke, he would say to me, "Approach the catch with the reverence you would approach God."

What Peter was talking about is "the catch," or the point of the stroke where the rower's body is compressed in a crouching position closest to the stern of the boat. The rower is balanced tenuously on their feet. The oars have just been carried over the water and are suspended in the air about to re-enter. This is a critical moment because the efficiency of the boat is in jeopardy. Any minor shift or movement has a direct impact on the rower's performance and the speed of the boat. If a single rower looses their balance at the catch, the boat could easily flip. When approaching the catch, it's not unusual to become tense in anticipation, causing the rower to suddenly rush the moving seat forward on the slides, to the catch. This is commonly known as "rushing the slide." Usually a coach would tell the rower to approach the catch by slowing down the movement of the seat. It seemed on this pilgrimage to Santiago, I was approaching the catch of my life and Peter's words reminded me to slow down and allow my journey to unfold.

People spend months and sometimes years preparing to walk a pilgrimage by researching history, routes, maps and the best equipment to address every possible scenario. I discovered, to embark on a pilgrimage, I really needed to consider three things: wear good walking boots, pack lightly and keep an open mind.

The definition of surrender suggests giving up or raising a white flag in defeat. On the Camino, I knew it was not possible to control the outcome of events that would unfold. Pilgrims were at the mercy of God, the people of Spain, the weather, the customs, the unknown truths of the path and their own physical and mental state. I thought if I was forced to accept the things I could not change, this would present an opportunity to learn the art of surrender. By surrendering to the Camino, it was a chance for me to flow naturally with the rhythm of the universe.

Although I had only recently decided to become a pilgrim, my pilgrim heart had been searching for a peaceful home from the time it left the safety of my mother's womb. Ever since then, I have been seeking to recapture the intensity of joy in absolute love. By accepting the Camino's spiritual quest to travel forward in a state of complete surrender, I would walk back to myself to become the authentic person I would recognize and know intimately. This was an essential feature of my journey which would begin with the first step I took on this pilgrimage.

5

a trickster appears

t's raining. The rain turns to hail. A strong wind howls, wrapping itself around the mountain side and completely ignoring me. Danger is all around. Everything I read about these mountains and what Jacques had said at the Pilgrim's Office, alerted me to the risk of climbing the Pyrenees in bad weather. To make matters worse, I chose to be completely alone, and I was. "Be careful what you wish for," I said to myself laughing aloud in disbelief as I took the first steps of my journey.

Climbing the mountain for hours weakened my legs. My lungs burn for more oxygen. The steep incline is grueling even for a trained athlete. I count ten steps and pause. In a state of complete exhaustion, Paul's words come to me, "Don't try so hard." I relax the death grip on my walking poles. Then almost effortlessly, the natural flow of the movement of walking begins to carry me forward. I am comforted by the thought rowers from the Argonaut Rowing Club crew and coach Paul are present in spirit. My crew's strength giving me the courage to press on. It is almost as if they are climbing with me each step of the way. As always, I am fully committed to this endeavor and I would never quit part way into a race or the Camino. I breathe deeply, filling my lungs with oxygen. This mountain is merely the first of many obstacles to be surmounted over the next twenty-nine days (virtually the same duration as a woman's cycle).

Unlike rowing in a crew, I am very much alone on my journey. I promise myself to stay committed to the present, resisting the desire to drag along the baggage of the past. I decide to embrace the idea that events on the Camino are not to be looked on as being good or bad, positive or negative, they just are.

All around me is barren land with short brown grass carpeting the rock underneath. As far as one can see, there are gray clouds and rugged mountain ranges and valleys. No buildings, no people, no animal life, only the mighty mountains. I am poised upon a plateau that rises almost 5000 feet from the valley below. The summit is near and a sense of peace and calmness comes with resting. I look out into the distant mountains thinking about Cebreiro and dreaming of the possibility of a miracle taking place on this mountain too. Then my eyes lock onto something much closer to me.

Set on the path immediately ahead is a pile of stones about waist high. The stones appear to be stacked in a deliberate manner. Many of them in various hues of gray with a touch of burnt orange; all different shapes and sizes. Fascinated by the idea that pilgrims before me have contributed to this rock cairn, I stop to admire its beauty. Removing my backpack, I set it down to begin looking for a stone to add to complete the ritual started by the pilgrims before me. Unable to find one in the immediate area, I'm forced to retrace the path before finally spotting a small stone. Picking it up with care, I carry my prized stone back, placing it on the very top. A feeling of hope fills me as I stare in wonderment at what has happened over time. This ritual is proof that past pilgrims sensed the same need for hope as I did. Hope that others had completed the uphill climb, even as they faced their fear. Hope that one is never alone on that part, or any part of the Camino. Hope that hope itself exists.

Questions started racing through my mind as I stood, the raging wind reminding me I still had 20 kilometers to finish before the end of that day. I should keep walking if I was going to make it to the safety of the refugio in Roncesvalles. I took a picture of the rock cairn to remind me when I got home that it was the strength of others, that gave me the courage to go on. Again, I could see that life on the Camino was not unlike rowing in a crew boat.

I had been walking for several hours, following the yellow arrows painted along the way; pointing the direction to San-tiago. I reached an intersection on the path where a yellow arrow couldn't be found. There were markings for the Euro-pean GR 65 hiking path but I did not know how to read them. After veering to the left path and walking almost a kilometer I came to a dead end. Discouraged, I turned around to walk back not sure about what to do. This was the first time I had become lost. Deciding it would be best to pause for a break, I sat down and removed my boots, hungrily eating yogurt and admiring the breathtaking scenery. I wished someone would come by, and sure enough I looked down the mountain path to see a pilgrim approaching. He was out of breath from scaling the steep incline and greeted me saying his name was

Karl, from Germany. According to Karl, we were the only pilgrims on the mountain that day. I asked if he knew which way to proceed. With the expertise of a seasoned hiker, he took out a map and quickly finding our location, confidently pointed to the path on the right.

I put my boots back on and we started walking together. Karl was in a hurry and his walking pace much faster than mine so it wasn't long before we separated with a friendly wave. I was experiencing my first introduction to the pilgrim's code, pleased to find it was perfectly acceptable to walk together in silence or to choose to walk alone. I liked the Camino already since one needn't be concerned about being seen as unsociable or rude should one chose either approach.

As a master rower, I discovered my maturing body required more recovery time than in the past so I took a break every two hours, whether I needed it or not. This reminded me to drink water to avoid dehydration and eat a snack to keep my energy charged. The next two hours passed quickly climbing the mountain and I was ready for a break. Resting within the silence of the clouds, I sat on the edge of the mountain in heavenly peace.

It was almost 2:00 p.m. and the weather was quickly changing, making me feel uneasy about finishing the rest of the journey that day. Seemingly out of nowhere, Karl appeared again. He could see that I was fighting the relentless gusty winds and suggested I take shelter with him further ahead, where we would be protected. A wet misty rain shower carried more cutting winds. I was nervous about the weather becoming worse, but grateful for Karl's company. We continued the steep ascent into the Pyrenees climbing in silence.

Walking through a forest, the path dropped quickly down the mountainside below for at least a thousand meters. Still not accustomed to the weight on my back, I feared I would just tip over and be gone forever. In the past, I wouldn't have considered being so afraid of this danger, but ever since my younger sister Donna died of cancer, I seem to have taken on some of her fears as my own. Strangely, it's as though there is a certain comfort associated with absorbing her fears on the Camino. Through the recognition of her emotion I am reminded of my love for Donna and I welcome the possibility of facing this demon for her. By agreeing to take on Donna's fears, I face them with an understanding that her soul would receive absolution from this burden. I question if this is my first pilgrim bargain with God.

Karl and I were walking faster to keep ahead of the quickly deteriorating weather. The summit arrived beneath our boots. A welcoming committee consisting of a flock of hawks, flew in a circle above us just as we arrived. It occurred to me, I had not seen many birds on the Camino. The view from the top was heavenly, and filled me with a quiet gentleness and an overall feeling of peace that I had never experienced before. Right away, the border to Spain appeared as a cattle grill that broke up a uniform line of fencing.

The descent was aggressive and hard on my knees even though I had walking poles to relieve some of the pressure. The weight of my pack swinging into my lower back with the declining landscape, felt like it was ripping the muscles in my knee with every step. The balls of my feet ached, then became an excruciating pain eventually forcing me to stop. I sat down and took off my boots to relieve my entire foot from the pressure. My enthusiasm had dwindled and left me in a miserable mood.

Returning to the path, I walked with Karl in my view just ahead of me, covering a distance of fourteen kilometers to the site where the famous city of Roncesvalles can be seen. Roncesvalles contains a beautiful, 13th century monastery where Agustinian monks have been caring for pilgrims for over 900 years. At one time it was a hospital for the pilgrims and even had its own burial grounds. After only seven hours of walking through the mountains, Karl and I had arrived in Roncesvalles. I was getting more excited about being in Spain and the prospect of staying in the comfort of the ancient Abbey was something to look forward to as well. Through the blue-gray mist, I caught the first glimpse of the medieval monastery that would be my home that night. It lay in the valley resting 1420 meters below the highest point on the mountain range. Consulting his map, Karl recommended to descend the Pyrenees via the path known as the *Route Napoleon*. Hoping that meant it would be short, at least. It was short all right, almost straight downhill. We were losing control and picking up speed as the sharp incline pulled us toward the village below. Heading down the steep path, we struggled in vain against the force of gravity. On the way Karl pointed out bunkers from the Spanish Civil War. Once we leveled off the city was in full view and walking seemed effortless. All physical pain subsided.

On our arrival, we were required to register at the office on the main floor. Since the refugio was not open for another half hour, we were just happy to be free of the burden of our backpacks as we sat down. The hospitalero, the person responsible for taking care of the pilgrims, arrived and welcomed us in Spanish. At least in France I could communicate a little but my attempts to learn Spanish from a CD had failed miserably. As luck would have it, Karl spoke adequate Spanish. It was expected we would attend a pilgrim's mass at 8:00 p.m. that evening to be followed by a traditional fish meal, the first supper.

One of my main reasons for this journey was to spend time alone. To have a spiritual journey unencumbered by social expectations. The fact I couldn't speak Spanish was appealing since it limited my conversations and kept me free from being distracted by other people's views and fears. On the Camino, I tried to avoid any dialogue about the religious aspects of this pilgrimage, making it perfectly clear to myself and others, this was my own personal spiritual journey. Determined not to have a dogmatic religious experience, I resisted being expected to go this Catholic pilgrim's mass. If I was forced to do something I didn't want to do in order to stay at the refugios, then I would consider staying in hotels along the way or better still, stop now and go home in protest.

In the meantime, the hospitalero escorted us up three flights of old, creaky, wooden stairs. They were worn down in the middle section from the constant wear and tear of pilgrim's shoes over the centuries. We entered a large room filled with bunk-beds. I immediately approached the far corner to be alone. Karl seemed to disappear off on his own. I unpacked my belongings, rolled out my sleeping bag and lay down on it, completely exhausted from the first day of climbing and breathing the fresh Camino air. With hands clasped behind my head and with a contented grin on my face, I became lost daydreaming about the events that had unfolded that day.

In the distance, I could hear the echo of heavy footsteps on the wooden stairs. Curious about who was arriving, I peered through the bunk-beds toward the door where a pilgrim stood. This man did not look like your typical modern day pilgrim. Alive with character, he was short, probably in his early fifties, wearing tight-fitting brown leather pants and a red bandanna tied around his neck. He scanned the room with the confidence of someone on a mission, his face softened by the colored light from the early evening sunset cast through the window.

His masculine features were wrapped in lightly bronzed skin that perfectly matched his dark hair. To me this suggested a Mediterranean heritage. He sported a blue backpack that listed to one side. A brown foam bedroll strapped on top of his backpack, gave the appearance that it was actually resting on his head. He needed a shave. With style, he swung a full length black umbrella forward as he walked. A grocery bag was in his other hand and a black leather pouch worn around his waist completed his ensemble.

I usually made an effort not to judge people by their appearance but with his character, I couldn't resist the temptation. I had made my verdict. I really hoped he would go to the other end of the refugio, far away from me but as if he was reading my mind, he immediately started to walk towards me. Throwing his backpack on the bottom bunk directly across from me, he spun around with the energy of a young man to acknowledge me with a big smile. He paused, taking a moment to assess the situation, then sat on the bed and grinned. Just imagining the implications of having this man sleeping in a bunk-bed directly across from me sent my imagination into a tail spin. It was usual for pilgrims to introduce themselves with their first name, followed their country of origin. "Hi, I'm Sue the Canadian," I blurted.

"I'm Dino, the Greek," he said with obvious pride. My face froze in shock. Questioning his intentions I immediately assumed if he was anything like my Greek ex-boyfriend, he was likely on the Camino not for salvation, but to find a woman who liked his leather pants. There I was judging again. Realizing what I was doing, I was disgusted by my attitude towards a complete stranger and a pilgrim. Whatever his reasons were for being there, I could already see this evening with Dino would test my intention to remain open and accepting of others.

Determined to keep a close eye on Dino I watched him, noticing how efficiently he moved through the ritual of unpacking. Each item was placed on the bed in a particular order with all of his belongings sorted neatly into plastic bags. With a cheeky grin, I asked him why he wore leather pants. With a very serious look, he said they were perfect for this journey because leather is natural and it breathes. He showed the concept by inhaling deeply and expanding his chest, and then he exhaled slowly adding that leather is also comfortable and maintains a constant body temperature. Dino asked why I was walking the Camino. I said that I wanted to spend time alone in order to figure out what I could contribute to the world in my lifetime. I didn't dare tell him I wanted to have a love affair with myself, for fear he might get the wrong idea.

Testing my pre-determined opinion, I smugly asked why he was on a pilgrimage. With sincerity and passion he said he viewed the pilgrimage as a form of discipline. I liked that reason and besides, Dino's theory fit perfectly into my training background as an athlete where I discovered nothing is achieved without committing to discipline. Even if I had talent, physical attributes, personality and Bill Gates's money, I might win races but if I didn't follow a disciplined program, I would never reach my true potential.

Dino wasn't finished with his lessons that day. He shared another profound idea with me. Speaking with a natural rhythmic flow to his voice he said, "On the Camino, some of us will become saints." I laughed nervously. Again I was resisting anything with a religious connotation. He sensed my quandary and said, "No, no, no, I am not talking about the meaning of a saint in a religious context, I'm talking about the real meaning of the word saint."

Anxiety tumbled about in my stomach as I was really being tested to remain open to his ideas. I failed at covering up my exasperation announcing in a sarcastic tone, "Well then, Dino, tell me, what is the real meaning of the word saint?"

His eyes locked onto mine and with a calm voice Dino said something to me that day, I would never forget. "A saint is someone who faces their fear."

Silence hung in the air between us.

I approach life from the position my destiny lies beyond my comfort zone. Somehow I knew if I truly wanted to live my destiny in life, on the Camino I would have to overcome my fear. Moved by Dino's words, I had never considered the possibility of becoming a saint. I wasn't a particularly good, unselfish person and definitely not pious, but secretly I always wanted to know what it would be like to be a saint.

A young woman of Peruvian descent arrived on the scene. She entered the bunkroom with the flare of an actress and introduced herself as "Shiva, from Calgary." Styled like a contemporary pilgrim, she was dressed in high-tech clothing with two oversized, thick, black braids that hung down either side of her head. Apparently the waist-length hair extensions were braided into her real hair relieving her of the ordeal of fussing with it. Since arriving by taxi from Pamplona, where she was visiting a friend, she had barely carried her backpack any distance, but felt it was already too heavy. She had overloaded it with power bars and power gel for extra energy that would be needed. Generously, she shared them with all of us.

In the far corner on the other side of the refugio, a pilgrim entered. He was a youthful and attractive man with long dirty blonde hair pulled back into a messy ponytail. With a reticent demeanor he walked slowly with his head downward. He wore faded jeans and plain running shoes, seemingly unprepared for a major walk. Shiva quickly announced, "His name is Stefan and he is 23 years old." I wondered why he was alone and before I could ask the question, Shiva went on to say she had heard he was a university student in Madrid. While there he heard about the Camino and because of some problems in a relationship with a girlfriend, he impulsively decided to walk.

The ancient stone walls of the monastery exuded a cool dampness with the onset of the evening air. Everything in the village was closed for the winter, so in an effort to stay warm, I decided to attend the pilgrim's blessing that evening afterall. Despite my misgivings, I would need all the prayers I could get whether I believed in the ceremony of the Catholic church or not.

Together Karl, Shiva, Dino, even the sullen Stefan, and I walked to the monastery together. As we entered the church, the dampness of the cold ancient stone hung in the darkness. The mystery of the ever present unknown was encouraging our little group to stay together, hanging onto the security of each other's presence. We fell into single file and proceeded to the first pew at the front of the church. Splitting into two groups, we took our places and I sat between Shiva and Dino. Stretching upright on the wooden pew, I tried to extend the sore muscles in my back.

Five priests arrived, one for each pilgrim. An older hunchbacked priest managing a slight limp, stepped forward to welcome us with a prayer. Then he announced the country of each pilgrim in attendance. Unable to understand the Spanish words spoken, my mind became empty while I listened to the music of the language, embracing the rhythm of the words. I looked around admiring the magnificence of the stained glass windows lost in the darkness outside. How beautiful the windows must appear in the softness of daylight, highlighting the French Gothic architecture of this gorgeous sacred structure.

Near the end of the service the older priest handed each of us a piece of paper with the *The Pilgrim's Prayer* typed in Spanish on one side and English on the other. We were invited to approach the altar for the final blessing bestowed on pilgrims. Everyone said the prayer together out loud. This was the same ritual that had been performed since the 12th century. A blessing from the Virgin Santa Maria de Roncesvalles offering to protect and defend the pilgrims on their journey.

Blessing and Prayer for the Pilgrim

Dear Lord Jesus Christ, who brought your servant Abraham out of the city of Caldeas protecting him through all his travels/wandering, and who was the Hebrew nation's guide through the desert, we ask you to bless these children of yours who, for the love they bear your name, are on a pilgrimage to Compostela.

Be for them their companion on the way, their guide at the cross-roads, their shelter on the road, their shade in the heat, their light in the darkness, their comfort in weariness and their resolve in intentions. So that through your guidance they arrive sound at the end of their road, and, enriched with grace and virtue, return home healthy and full or worthy virtues.

In the name of Jesus Christ our Lord. March in the name of Christ who is the way, and pray for us in Compostela.

It was incredibly special for me to receive Santa Maria's blessing on the Camino. The entire focus of the religious aspects of the pilgrimage until this point, had been about St. James. Most of the stories I read were about priests, male saints and male pilgrims of the past, known as peregrinos. Even the word *peregrina* used to address a female pilgrim is hardly ever used. And the most celebrated worldly woman of the Camino, Chaucer's Wife of Bath, is barely known as a pilgrim. In the 12th century the women on the Camino traveled with their husbands, never alone. Although women were believed to bring an increased level of devotion, they were often not permitted in monastic sanctuaries. I was comforted by the

Virgin's presence and felt honored by her worthiness. As a mother of three daughters, walking the Camino alone, I welcomed her maternal blessing offered to defend me from the perils to my soul and body. It was as though my mother was present and through her spirit, I was prepared to embark further on my Camino.

The priests spoke the final words, "And pray for us when you reach Santiago." I smiled inwardly realizing this was the currency of the Camino. A barter of sorts that implies when something is done for a pilgrim, then the pilgrim returns the favor by carrying intentions to Santiago. It is also customary to ask a pilgrim to give a hug to the statue of St. James the Apostle in Santiago.

My eyes came to rest on the altar which led me to look upward at a gorgeous 14th century statue of the Madonna, seated peacefully with her Son on her lap. She is known as "The Virgin of Roncesvalles." Legend has it that the statue of the Virgin Mary and her son were found buried on this very spot. The monastery was built to commemorate the miraculous finding. It was comforting for me to be in the presence of another woman, a Mother, as a blessing.

Without warning, all the lights went out except for one spotlight on the statue. The priests began to sing a hymn, moving me to tears. I hadn't been to mass or a blessing in years and now my Catholic upbringing had been triggered, releasing the emotion of fear as I stood there in the church. Somehow after the blessing was finished, the fear dissipated leaving me with a divine feeling of overall peace. My mind was opening to the possibility of considering there might be more to this journey. By expecting nothing I believed everything was a gift.

I was deeply moved.

I looked around with a renewed sense of presence, wondering what had driven centuries of virgin pilgrims to walk the Camino. Many before me had also been blessed by the Virgin Mary and eaten the pilgrim's fish meal in anticipation of the beginning of a new life journey. What had they learned? What had they experienced? Our humble group walked from the church, all somewhat dazed by the mystical nature of the service, to the restaurant for a traditional pilgrim's meal. As the only patrons that winter evening, we had exceptional service. Dino, not surprisingly, took charge of ordering my meal since he could speak some Spanish. The wine arrived and we raised our glasses to a safe journey. The meal included soup, whole trout, potatoes and a custard flan for dessert. It was delicious but I missed the French bread already.

We ate and shared stories about our lives back home. When I mentioned I had three teenage daughters, Dino asked if I was married. When I said no, he tilted his head back and smirked. I just ignored him.

It is said that everyone has a love affair on the Camino

I didn't come all this way for a love affair with a man, I could find that at home. My journey would be a spiritual awakening to the discovery of self-love and I was certain there was no possibility of a romantic encounter in the offing. I was as certain of this as I was that my spiritual journey would not have a religious component to it either.

6

zen and the art of rowing

*F*inally, the meal was finished and we walked back to the Abbey. I was emotionally and physically exhausted from the events of the day. I was too tired to be sociable and only half-listened to the stories from the pilgrims I had met, preferring to occupy my mind with the realities of the immediate future; the potential for inclement weather, possible injuries, blisters, lack of food or water, getting lost, finding shelter, wild dogs and sleeping next to Dino.

Despite all that, a deep sleep followed. Waking up the next morning, Roncesvalles looked like a winter wonderland. Almost twenty centimeters of snow had fallen during the night. Beholden to our schedules, but concerned about safety, Dino, Karl, Shiva and I left the monastery together deciding to take the route along the road. We knew it would be impossible to see the yellow arrows on the path in the forest under the newly-fallen snow. Stefan, the aloof young student, went alone on the other path through a Navarre forest.

I walked alone, although I always kept the other pilgrims within sight. My focus for the first hour was spent walking with the intention of becoming more aware of my present state of self-love. It seemed there was a higher consciousness evoked with each breath I took. As I walked, I repeated all my intentions determined to make them a reality.

Later that morning I met up with Dino and found myself glad to see him. We talked about the physical demands of the journey. Then Dino said something to me that made a lot of sense. "On the Camino," he said, "we will recreate our bodies and recreate our minds."

I chuckled saying, "Dino, I understand the idea of recreating our bodies because I'm an athlete and I know that when you train you can change your muscle structure but as far as recreating our mind, how are we going to do that?" Dino assured me that through the thoughts and the intentions we make along the way, our minds will be recreated based on what we are thinking. I had already defined my intentions as my earnest desires, repeating these thoughts allowed me to establish a discipline that would be recognized by my body, mind and spirit. If Dino was right, my intention to have a love affair with myself, along with the other intentions I had stated, would be fulfilled.

Even with this discipline engaged, my mind jumped back to the same thoughts over and over again. Soon I was thinking about my daughters, hoping they were managing through their life's journey back home. Reliving scenarios that had long since passed, I wondered how I could be a better parent for them. Then rowing came into my thoughts again. It was such a significant part of my life before I left for the Camino, I couldn't let go of the people or the experiences that often came to mind.

I also thought about one of the most significant experiences of my life. It began on August 30, 2001. We were in Montreal, at the rowing course that was built for the 1976 Olympics. The night before the FISA World Master's Rowing Championships, Paul had called the entire women's master crew together to impart some motivational words and to review the race strategy. A sense of wonderment showed on the face of every athlete as they arrived, awkwardly finding a seat at the boardroom table. Paul moved to the front of the room and stood there until a respected hush silenced all conversation. With the authority bestowed upon great coaches, the rowers became attentive to the words about to be spoken.

Intellectually one would think winning a race was dependent on the ability of the crew to row technically fast, along with the skill of a coxswain to be able to steer the course and call an exceptional race. As experienced competitive rowers under the guidance of Paul's coaching philosophies, each had learned from past experiences that rowing a fast stroke was the easy part. Fortunately Paul had instilled in us his vision for a unique crew. "By contributing all that each rower can, with a technical excellence bordering on perfection in performance levels, it is not only teamwork, but a passion for oneself, your crew and your dream that makes the difference." We focused on values such as honesty, courage, commitment, pride, honor and determination. "Without these values," he told us, "the crew is extremely vulnerable." He would frankly say that in his view, winning a gold medal was a poor goal for anyone.

Paul continued his address to the crew and to my surprise, for the first time I didn't actually listen to the words he was saying. Instead I felt the intensity of his passion and love for the sport and more importantly, the individuals in the room. I could see he was intent on putting the right focus into the minds of the athletes, to create his idea of unified passion.

Now I listened to his words as he spoke. Just as the parachute instructor asked us to forget everything we had learned during training, Paul asked us to forget everything we had accomplished in the sport of rowing up until that time. He said that we should forget the medals we had won and lost, forget accomplishments, forget the failures and goals yet accomplished, and forget the past. As he spoke my mind wandered thinking about the medals I had won and the thousands of hours of work I had put into training. I learned the sport of rowing at the age of 40 and here I was less than six years later, rowing for my country in a crew about to race for a world title. By carefully organizing my lifestyle, I had made my contribution to the team by being the strongest link that was possible for me. In making this commitment, I asked myself if I was prepared to surrender personal and public acknowledgment of my accomplishments. Did I trust his judgment as a coach enough to do something so unconventional as to forget everything I had worked to achieve?

I had trained and made sacrifices in my life to reach this level of athletic competition and I was very proud of my success. I knew Paul was right about letting go to completely surrender to the boat but in a world that honors material values and goals, I desperately wanted to hold onto the memory of my achievements. In case we didn't win the race, I knew I could always go back to resting on my laurels.

Paul was asking every one of us to let go of the past. It didn't take me long to decide to forfeit what I thought was self-pride for the sake of the boat's shared experience. Paul wanted us to create what he called, "A majestic team." He also had another name for our superannuated crew that wasn't quite as flattering. With a true fondness for each of the rowers on the crew he called us, "The Fossils."

He walked slowly over to the pad board and began to write the words; "Create From This Moment On." Everyone sat motionless, unsure about how to react to this message. By way of explanation, he said what happened in the past, is gone forever. There is nothing that we could change. He assured us that holding onto those memories did not contribute in any way to our ability to create what we truly desired that day. And since we have no idea what the future would hold, why would we spend any time thinking about what it would be like to win the medal?

"This moment is different," he said, "each of you have the ability to create a crew with a unified vision and passion from this moment on."

Paul believed we could create our future and we believed him. Besides, he had just set a peerless example to follow by leaving his ego at home. For me, Paul's request meant facing my fear and truly letting go of all control. Paul spoke with passion in his voice and therefore I readily accepted letting go of my ego for the sake of the crew. We all made the choice that evening to embrace the vision and values he presented. It was this choice that created an elite caliber rowing crew.

This sport involved rowing on water as well as many levels of cross-training on the ergometer, with weights, aerobics, cycling, running and more. Paul allowed us to decide how we wanted to cross train, as long as we followed the required training schedule. I chose to do yoga. I loved Bikram Yoga, which involved doing 26 postures, repeated twice and held for one minute each. To add to the intensity, the yoga class is held in a room heated up to 110 degrees Fahrenheit. It is a unique offering of aerobic, flexibility and strength training. More importantly, it allowed me to develop a disciplined balance of mind, body and soul. At the end of each class we spent time meditating, manifesting our intentions and desires with a clear mind. Over time my rowing technique improved and I had evolved to incorporating a spiritual approach to this physically demanding sport.

Less than a month prior to today's race, our master's crew raced in the open category for the provincial championships, competing against members of Canada's national team and the top varsity crews. As Master's rowers we were accustomed to rowing 1000 meters, which is like a long sprint, but Paul wanted to test our tenacity by placing us in open competition, where the races were 2000 meters and required a very different race strategy.

We had a great start and it was just before we were going to face the section of the row known as "the wall" (about 1200 meters into the race). While rowing I began to experience a unique oneness with the crew, the boat and the water. All thoughts were cleared from my mind as I moved into a sense of timelessness. The coxswain's voice was distant and muffled as she pushed us further than we thought possible. I was pushed to the end no longer able to feel the intense physical demands on my body. We were rowing at a very fast rate of 36 strokes per minute, pressing about 45 lb. pressure with each stroke.

With an ethereal sense, I became aware that I had risen out of my body. I was watching the crew from above and I saw myself rowing, leaving me with a sense of elation and pride as I looked down. Suddenly, realizing that I was out of my body and out of the boat, I worried that Paul or the crew would see me slacking off so I immediately returned to my physical body. Not knowing how much time had passed or how I did that, I returned to focusing on rowing the race. The physical agony experienced at the end of a 2000 meter race returned, physically depleting the strength in every muscle of my body. It was a profound experience for me to discover I had the ability to leave my physical body during the most crucial part of a race and still contribute to the boat.

Back at the racecourse for the FISA World Master's Rowing Championships, the crew was now mentally and physically prepared. In a state of surrender, we were all free to align with the power of the rowers to carry each other down the course, without hesitation about anyone's commitment to the boat. It was as though Paul had removed all the negative race day pressure. He left us with the idea that we had the ability to create something special and by tapping into the power of all nine women as a whole, we were unbeatable.

The next day we met with Paul under a tree and he had very little to say. We walked over to our boat. With the precision of an expertly trained crew, intense, yet liberated in some way, we carried the boat down to the water. I honestly can't remember what I thought about as we rowed to the starting gate, except that I had a feeling that I was a part of something powerfully unique. Every cell in my body had been trained to work on the command of the coxy. Each of the rowers in the boat had specific roles that were determined by the seat they occupied. Each of the seats in the boat were numbered from bow to stern, from One to Eight. I rowed in Two seat, near the front of the boat. This was a technical position where I partnered with bow seat (One seat) to keep the boat set up. This would allow stroke pair (Seven and Eight seat) the best platform possible from which to set the cadence of the stroke. It also helped to support the four rowers (seats Three, Four, Five and Six) in the middle of the boat, known as "the engine room," to do their job.

Waiting at the starting line for the official to call our boat seemed to take forever. As Two seat, I was responsible for "touching up" a technique of scooping a bit of water with the oar, just enough to adjust the bow of the boat to remain perfectly aligned with the course. The race was called halfway through touching up. I quickly moved my oar into position, the coxy called our attention and the race began. Three minutes and forty-two seconds later we crossed the finish line, first! It wasn't just technical speed that took us to the finish; we had created a unique crew with vision, cleanly rowing past all other crews to win the gold medal. Each member of our crew recognized the profound journey had not ended in winning a medal.

Stroke by stroke, I became one with the crew. Step by step, I was becoming one with the Camino. Stone by stone, I would become one with myself.

7

stone by stone

icholas Flamel is another legend of the Camino, and more recently of *Harry Potter* fame. As an exceptionally renowned alchemist who was active in the late 14th century, he made the pilgrimage to Santiago. It is said that when he traveled, he met a Master of the Kabbalah, referred to as Abraham the Jew, who taught him the secret of the Philosopher's Stone. As long as he was in possession of the stone, he believed he would have eternal life. I wondered where the stone was now?

I was walking alone again. It had been snowing earlier that day with a strong wind that threatened to blow me over as I made the ascent from the last mountain of the Pyrenees to eventually arrive in the medieval town Puenta la Reina. This city is famous for it's magnificent 11th century picturesque bridge with six arches crossing over the river Arga. The bridge was built by the Navarrese Queen so pilgrims could avoid being robbed or drowned by the ferrymen. I continued past the vineyards, eating wine grapes along the way tasting the flavor indicative of the Navarre region. I had pulled muscles in my knee that nagged constantly throughout the day, made worse from an injury caused when I slipped on the snow leaving Roncesvalles. The pain was excruciating and I was moving slowly and favoring my knee. My mind was mesmerized by the movement of the huge white windmills on the horizon that acted as a point of reference marking the distance I had yet to cover.

Over the last few days, the activity of walking up to eight hours a day with eleven kilograms on my back had conditioned my body. My mind struggled, particularly frustrated with the same tedious thoughts repeating themselves. The solitary time was becoming boring. Incensed with the banality of the simple thoughts in my mind I began to question every aspect, including the meaning of my life. With each question asked, more thoughts stirred. As more thoughts arose, more questions needed to be asked and answers sought. A vicious cycle. Desperate for peace, I tried different ways to distract my mind. For many hours, I counted each step until I reached one hundred and then started counting from one again. This was as boring as the meager thoughts plodding haphazardly through my mind but at least it passed the time. I also found myself singing the same song, *Smile and the World Smiles with You*.

Anger and disappointment started to build. My stomach ached, my head pounded, my knee was on fire and I was downright cranky. Wallowing in my own misery, I thought it was a good thing that I chose to walk alone. No one would want to be around someone so ill-tempered. I wished to be alone and I was alone. Next time I will be more careful about my wishes. Suddenly, I just stopped walking. Standing in the middle of the path, seconds seemed to pass like minutes. Ideas sped through my mind as I considered how I could get myself out of this ridiculous situation, wanting to pack it in and go home.

Where were the buses that everyone talked about? I was at least ten kilometers from the nearest town, which meant another three hours before I could get to a phone. Why hadn't I brought my cell?

Paralyzed, I pondered the outcome of my actions if I didn't take another step. Looking ahead towards the mountains it occurred to me that I would not reach them as long as I just stood there. No movement, plus no action, equals no result. I started to think about what I was committed to in my life. This reminded me of a conversation I had at home with friends about commitment. They asked me how I stayed committed for 38 days to tryout for the rowing crew. I described what went on in my mind. I have a visual image of a door that sits just behind my right ear. Each time my commitment wavers, the door will open a crack letting in excuses to use as backup. Once the excuses come into my mind, then it's almost impossible to get them out the door. Alternatively, by keeping the excuse door closed, the excuses cannot enter and all my energy is focused on making the crew, not on making excuses. This was my way of being aware of my fear.

As I stood on the path, I knew that it didn't matter what ideas I had in my mind about getting to Santiago, if I didn't start walking I would never arrive anywhere. I stared at the long empty road ahead of me. Standing with my shoulders rounded forward in defeat, I resolved if I just put one foot in front of the other, I would reach Cebreiro. My thoughts shifted to the intention of arriving at my destination. Just as my perspective changed, suddenly I didn't feel alone on the Camino anymore. I wasn't alone. I could see hundreds of tiny white bubbles all around me, seemingly like angels dancing.

I thought I was going crazy and I hadn't been to the Meseta yet. Then I remembered a special gift I received that night at Hernando's Hideaway in Toronto. Donna had kept her promise sending 2000 angels with me on my journey. It was timely they'd appeared just when I needed them most. With a concerted effort, I took one step and then another. Soon a familiar rhythm returned and once again I was on my way.

It was Sunday, a day of rest, maybe for the corporate world and a certain deity, but I walked 22 kilometers. Arriving at the refugio early in the afternoon, I was fatigued by the gusty wind and my constantly nagging knee injury. While signing the guest book I noticed a message to me from Kristin, a fellow Canadian and rower who was about six days ahead of me on the walk. Such a delightful surprise. As I rested, I heard a familiar voice speaking and I looked over to the doorway to see the trickster, Dino the Greek. He strolled in the room still sporting his leather pants, but this time with his boots hanging around his neck. I was shocked to see he was barefoot. He announced that he had been walking all day without his shoes and socks. When he was in the army back home in Greece, they used to go walking in bare feet because it engaged different muscles in the foot taking the strain off already overworked ones. He boasted that he still takes long journeys barefoot, touting the benefits of natural reflexology as a bonus.

Dino unpacked his groceries and cracked open a bottle of wine, sharing it with everyone there. Standing with his chest forward and his glass held high he called out, "To love, to time and may we have lots of both to enjoy." Then Karl, Stefan and Dino went outside to get wood to build a fire in the oversized fireplace. We all hung our clothes on a makeshift clothesline also provided by Dino, the ever-resourceful peregrino. The wine relaxed me. Resting on the top bunk with my little red diary, I began to write the events that unfolded that day. I thought about how this journey had provided me the time to enjoy the simple pleasures of the pilgrim life.

By following a routine for packing each morning, I was less likely to forget something. I woke up each day at the same time, drank a bottle of water, ate yogurt and then I packed my things. By seven o'clock, I was outside walking under the stars of the Milky Way, prepared to begin that day's journey. Religiously, I spent the first hour of each day in a state of awareness, intending to learn self-love. While walking, I would repeat the intentions I had written down in my diary. During the last kilometer of the day, I walked in a state of gratitude, considering the things I was thankful for that day. This completed the cycle of daily rituals as the ceremony of my pilgrimage.

For some reason on this day I noticed neat piles of stones placed on the edge of the path. Often they were left on the top of the concrete markers that were decorated with a blue tile imbedded with a scallop shell symbol that indicated the way to Santiago. I assumed the piles of stones were placed by the pilgrims before me and wanting to be a part of a historic ritual, I added a stone of my own. Even though I did not understand why I did this, I felt like I was a part of something very special.

Next morning, I arrived at a small village that looked as if nothing had changed in centuries. With a deliberate pace, I walked in time to the sound of my walking sticks tapping on the cobblestone road. A man called to me from a window on the second floor of a house, reminding me of catcalls I heard when I was young, coming from construction workers on the streets of Toronto. Calling out to me he repeated "Sancti-temple" or something that sounded similar to that. I thought he was referring to a church and not wanting to ignore his request, I nodded my head in agreement, although I was not sure what I was agreeing to. He motioned for me to wait there and a minute later, a short, jovial man appeared in the front doorway, bearing a large iron key in his hand. Using sign language coupled with some simple Spanish he managed to communicate where the church was, sending me there with the key. I marveled at the trust people along the Camino placed in strangers.

Carefully I slipped the key into the lock, opening the old wooden door. It creaked loudly, echoing through the hollow space. I tiptoed into the church feeling I should be respectfully quiet. Standing in awe of the statues and paintings of the saints, I was reminded of Dino's words that a saint is one who faces their fear. I lit three candles; one for my mother, one for my three daughters and one for Luba and Vince, close friends of mine who had lost their sixteen-year-old son in a car accident. Then I knelt down, easing onto my sore knee to pray. A woman came in the back door and thanked me for opening the church. Leaving some money in the donation box, I quietly left.

It was a gorgeous sunny day. The terrain was easy to walk with only one small mountain range to challenge. Around 3:00 p.m. I arrived in the city of Estella; which means, "star" in Spanish. Located at the point where the Camino Frances meets with the Camino Arles route joining the two paths to Santiago, it brings pilgrims from different routes together.

The next day I left in the stillness of the morning to walk 22 kilometers alone. I arrived at the Los Arcos refugio to find

Stefan, another German, Andreas, Petra, from Holland, Karl, Shiva and Dino. There were no cooking facilities available so we decided to go out together for a pilgrim's meal at a local restaurant. An Austrian couple joined us at a round table for a warm meal and lively chatter. Since everyone was from a different country, the conversation was a feast of many languages. Luckily for me, someone was always able to translate. During dinner, I thought about the stone cairns I had seen on the path. When the conversation stopped, I asked if anyone at the table knew the reason for the piles of stones along the way. Sitting directly across from me, Andreas the German pilgrim smiled with anticipation and told me he knew a story about the stones. I asked him to share it with me.

"It is said, if you pick up a stone and put some of your sorrow into it, when you place the stone down you leave your sorrow behind."

I was moved. The story resonated with me. If I could leave my sorrow on the Camino, surely it would create more space in my heart for love. The next day, as soon as I went outside to begin walking, the first thing I did was pick up a stone. I was not sure how to do this, so I just imagined I could put sorrow into the stone. Holding the stone in my hand as I walked, I caressed the smooth edges with my fingers like I was rubbing the sorrow into the stone. Then I carefully set the stone down on the side of the path, letting go of my sorrow with it. Almost immediately, my heart opened up for more love and it felt so good that I wanted to pick up another stone right away. So I did but this time I thought about putting the sorrow of my daughters into the stone. Seeing a small round stone, I picked it up for my oldest daughter Tara. I held it for a while as I walked, putting her sorrow into it and then I placed it down on another stone. The next stone I picked up was for middle daughter Meghan. I held the stone close to my heart imagining her sorrow was moving into the stone, and then I gently placed it down. Finally, I picked up a stone for Simone, my youngest daughter. With intention, I put her sorrow into the stone too. It was perfect. This soon would become a ritual too.

The first stone I picked up each day was for me. Then I would pick up stones for my daughters, mother, family and friends. Whenever anyone came to my mind as I walked, I picked up a stone in their name, placing it down on the Camino. Never at any time did I suppose I knew exactly what their sorrow was, I only knew they possessed it. This was my secret gift to them. Performing this ritual would allow me to understand that through my own sorrow, and the sorrow of others, I could expand my capacity for love.

As long as I had possession of a stone, like Nicholas Flamel the famous alchemist, I believed I would have eternal life.

the honor of being a pilgrim

*H*ow is it that someone can peer into the life of another, add some ingredient and like a pinch of salt to completely change the flavor of that which is already being savoured?

It was raining, a cold mist leaking a chill into my bones that left my body filled with tension. I was reminded of the time I suffered hypothermia. It was a few years ago and I was rowing with a group of women training for the Head of the Charles regatta, a five-kilometer race in Boston, Massachusetts, USA. In mid-October, we were on Lake Ontario during dusk doing mock-up races to test our speed and endurance under race conditions. Already 14 minutes into a race piece, we had rowed over four kilometers at a very high stroke rate. The coxy yelled the commands to motivate through the final strokes before the finish. The boat was set up beautifully, perfectly balanced, something very difficult to do with eight rowers and a coxy in a boat that is 60 feet long and has a round hull. As expected, our cumulative source of energy was beginning to deplete, but we were determined to set a record time.

Without any warning, my oar was yanked out of my hands, jabbing into the section below my ribs with a force that picked me up out of my seat, tugging my feet from the shoes tied into the bottom of the boat, I was thrown like a rag doll over the side of the boat into the freezing cold waters of Lake Ontario. Norma, sitting in bow seat followed landing on top of me and pushing me further underwater. We don't wear life jackets while rowing so it was more of a risk for us if we accidentally entered the water. I remembered the life saving warning learned many years ago, that a drowning person would grab onto anyone near them and take them down too. Because of this, I purposely swam away from her.

The wind had been knocked out of me and I needed to come up for air. I gasped and turned around, now wanting to swim toward the boat. Using a calm voice I encouraged Norma to the side of the boat, where the crew could console her. Finally a coach boat came over and we managed to climb into it and we made our way back to the rowing club. Later, I learned the University of Toronto varsity men's heavyweight crew, who were also rowing at a high rate had accidentally collided head on with our boat.

Unaware that I was suffering from exposure and shock, it took two days for my body to recover as I went through various stages of extreme heat and shivering cold body temperatures. When I arrived at the refugio that night, wet and cold, the residual effects of exposure were triggered, leaving me physically and emotionally weakened.

The next morning at the refugio I moved around swiftly packing my belongings with an efficiency I had mastered from repeating the same tasks over and over. I thought I was the first one up, but when I went into the kitchen Brigitte the Austrian was already there fixing breakfast. The smell of fresh coffee lingered. Her round, jovial face grinned at me warmly. I admired her skin that was kissed with a golden tan acquired from the endless hours spent walking outdoors over several weeks. "Buenos dias, eh!" I said in my limited Spanish with a Canadian accent. Her attractive features glowed as she laughed in a teasing manner. She was full of love and life I wanted to hug her but for some reason I resisted.

Preparing her breakfast, Brigitte maneuvered about gracefully in the unfamiliar room with the expertise of a woman who had obviously spent years in a kitchen. I marveled at her precision while thinking there was something special about the spirit of this woman whose tiny muscular body seemed to be carrying the weight of a heavy soul. One never knows what a pilgrim is actually carrying in their personal backpack.

Without effort our light conversation deepened into one you might experience speaking to a life-long friend. Brigitte talked about her desire to live a life of purpose. As a seasoned pilgrim who had already walked for six weeks, I admired her tenacity wanting to know what really drove this woman's desire to walk from Le Puy, France. She'd already been walking for over a month. Even though she appeared to be content, there was a deep sorrow reflected in her eyes. Taking me into her confidence she shared with me her reasons for walking. Like me she preferred to work through her personal life issues on her own rather than going to someone for professional help.

As a pilgrim who had walked many more miles than me, Brigitte garnered my respect and admiration. I listened attentively to every word she spoke. Without prompting, as though compelled to speak the words within her, she began to describe her observations of my qualities. As she spoke, my body remained completely still and open trying to avoid the possibility of missing an important part of her message.

"Sue, you have a special voice. It's full, without any shyness about what you want to say. It comes through very naturally. I can see that you love people and there is something very, very special you will share with them from this journey on the Camino. Go and speak."

Brigitte's words assured me I was now following another type of Camino arrow to find the way. It was like she was a mirror held up to my soul, reflecting back to me that which I couldn't see for myself. To my surprise she had described the type of person I wanted to be. I adored her. I finished my coffee and rose to leave. I gave her a warm hug and called out the pilgrim's salute, "Buen Camino," saddened that I might never see her again. Returning to the bunkroom I dressed in layers wearing my headband and mitts for warmth. I stepped out into the cold and I again looked for a yellow arrow to guide me.

Once onto the busy streets of city of Logrono I was catapulted into the realities of city life. The traffic seemed to be moving incredibly fast. Everyone appeared to be hurrying. I had been walking at a rate that covered four kilometers an hour. It had slowed my approach to life considerably, making it seem odd that people were actually rushing. I saw a stone and picked it up for Brigitte. Holding it in my hand, I put her sorrow into the stone, hoping she would find peace and love in her life. This was my gift to her.

In the city I sometimes became disoriented because it was difficult to find the yellow arrows. Twice that day I got lost.

Stopping at a bank machine I took out 50,000 pesetas and then visited a Panaderia to buy fresh bread, sheep cheese and Morcella for lunch. After packing the food in the top pouch of my backpack, I swung it over my shoulders, snapped the buckles into place before pulling the straps on my shoulders to a comfortable position. I walked out ready for the next pilgrim experience.

Opening the door, my eyes immediately started to scan the office buildings across the street looking for a yellow arrow. Confused with the rush hour commotion, I paused on the sidewalk trying to gather my composure. Looking down the street I noticed a woman standing outside the door of another store staring at me. It was as though she was waiting for me to see her. My eyes were immediately attracted to her hands that indicated hardship and aging, presumably from a long life caring for the family and home. They were clasped tightly together as though she was holding a rosary in prayer. Dressed completely in black, she was short, with dark hair pulled back in a bun to expose dark brown canny eyes. There was a sudden calmness all around me, as though time and traffic had stood still.

Once assured she had my complete attention, she looked directly into my eyes and made the sign of the cross, blessing herself with the reverence one would do so in front of an altar. She put her hands together again and kissed them bending her head forward toward me, as if in worship. Without hesitation, she quickly disappeared into the crowds of people rushing to work. I stood unable to move, completely in awe of her display of respect towards a simple pilgrim. Was Our Lady of Roncesvalles watching over me? That day, in a city called Logrono, I learned about the honor of being a pilgrim and I was humbled.

clarity of vision

On seven days God created Heaven and Earth and had a day of rest too. In seven days I had walked 200 kilometers but there was no rest for me.

Yesterday I walked 31 kilometers to reach the town of Redecillia. Many of the refugios are closed in the winter season which sometimes left me no choice about the distance I would have to walk, but the Camino had a way of making things unfold perfectly.

Before leaving the refugio in Redecillia early that morning, Stefan and I agreed to meet at the first bar we came to in Santo Domingo de la Calzada, a village named after a renowned Benedictine monk who devoted his life to serving pilgrims in the 11th century. Beyond this village, lay another desolate 12 kilometer section of the Camino before it turns into the mysterious, allegedly madness-inducing Meseta.

I had been walking for so many hours each day it remained a challenge for me to focus on the present moment. Earlier in the week, I severely twisted my ankle climbing on slippery rocks. Angered and frustrated because it not only added another entry to my existing list of injuries, the pain also distracted me from staying focused on my intentions. In desperation, I found myself bartering with God again, promising that if I made it to Santiago, I would serve people in some way.

Even as I barter, the truth remains that I am accountable and responsible for all my actions to create the future I desire. Walking every day, I became conscious of how I used physical discomfort as a ploy to deny myself love. Every time I got close to surrendering to self-love, I was distracted by some form of physical pain or illness. Unsure of the mechanics behind this association, I decided that if I try to notice how love presents itself within me, my awareness will at least provide me with a choice of how to react.

It was now sunny and the temperature hovered around a relatively balmy six degrees. There was no one around for miles so at least I could tuck into a bush and go to the bathroom in privacy. Unlike the time I sauntered onto an empty farmer's field and casually squatted in the open air, without a worry that I would be seen. Just as I was finished and about to stand up, I looked up to see a huge tractor stopped directly in front of me with a man sitting at the driver's wheel. He looked at me in embarrassed shock. At the same time we both tried to look away quickly pretending we did not know what had just taken place, but it was too late. All I could do was laugh at myself. I stood turning away to do up my pants and I walked back to the road laughing hysterically out loud. I was reminded of the earliest lesson I had learned on my journey; you are never alone on the Camino.

When I first started walking the Camino, my thoughts were disjointed and scattered. Habitually I would go back to thoughts that had been repeated in my mind day after day.

Today, I was beginning to think more about the life I truly wanted to create for myself, although seriously concerned about integrating the experiences on the Camino with the world back home.

Over the last year I'd spent considerable time dedicated to developing awareness and new skills to live in the present moment. Marcia's workshop had presented the theory that if we were genuine and present at all times, we would say the right words, do the right things and always have the right answers that were perfect for that moment in time. Intuitively, I knew there were many questions that I needed answered. What I did not know is, what were the questions I needed to ask? I believed if I was patient as I walked, the questions would come to me and if I were present and in the moment, I would have the right answers within me. Rather like a transcendental Jeopardy Game show.

By focusing my attention on a spot that I could not see in the space ahead of me I meditated on it. This provided a unique form of discipline that allowed me to clear my mind completely in meditation and then walk into the present moment; the place where my future is created. Reminding me that the Sufi's believed the way to mindfulness of the essential self is through awareness as the balance between activity and surrender. It was clear to me, the more I walked, the more I became aware.

Shortly after noon I arrived in Santo Domingo and went directly to the first bar to find that Stefan was not there. That was odd because he usually walked faster than me. Not wanting to waste precious daylight, I chalked it up to his solitary nature and left. I went to the Cathedral to see one of the earliest Gothic constructions in Spain.

On my way I stopped to buy juice. The shopkeeper asked, in broken English, if I was going to see the live chicken and hen on display at the Cathedral. "Sorry," I said, "I don't know anything about it." That was all he needed to hear. Excitedly, he told the story about a famous miracle that happened in the 16th century. He said, there was a young man traveling with his parents on the road to Santiago. They arrived at this village where the innkeeper's daughter attempted to make advances to him without success. Seeking revenge for being rebuffed, she put a silver mug in the pilgrim's pack. She then informed her father the mug was missing, saying she had last seen the pilgrim with it. The silver mug was found in the young man's possession and he was declared guilty of stealing. Against the pleas of his parents for mercy, he was strung up on gallows and left to die.

Somewhere on their way back from Santiago his parents heard their son's voice calling to them. Obviously, surprised that he was still alive they decided to make a final attempt to get their son back. The parents went to the judge to beg for his freedom. The judge was just sitting down to a chicken dinner when he proclaimed, "That boy is no more alive than these birds on my plate." And with that, the birds stood up and started to crow. The judge immediately released the pilgrim and in celebration of the miracle, live chickens have been displayed at the Cathedral in an elegant cage ever since. "It is said," the shopkeeper assured me, "if the chicken clucks or crows to a pilgrim, it brings good luck."

The site of the Cathedral was breathtaking. The building had been started in the 11th century and was built, stone by stone, over almost 500 years. Entering the Cathedral to see the interior, I was completely taken by its beauty. My heart beat faster in the presence of such an astounding mystical place of worship. Kneeling at a pew in the back of the church, I said a prayer in thanks. Then I proceeded to see the famous chickens in the ornate golden cage. Standing there, they didn't cluck, crow or even look at me. Disappointed, I left.

An impressive separate Baroque tower rises over the village. There was a lot of activity in the main square, as preparations were underway for the upcoming Christmas season. People worked busily to set up market stalls and a decorative nativity scene. For the first time, I wished I could stay in the village to experience this local culture and celebration. I reminded myself that I was not there to celebrate local customs; I was committed to a spiritual journey to my soul and so I must continue walking.

The spiritual solitude of the Camino gave me the freedom to be aware of the very source of my soul. I longed to share this discovery with another pilgrim who would understand so I returned to the first bar in the village to see if Stefan had arrived. Sure enough, he was sitting at a table near the window. We greeted each other like old friends. Stefan went to the bar to get a café con leche (espresso with milk) for each of us while I removed my boots and socks. I could feel hot spots on the bottom of my feet, a warning sign that blisters could be developing. I was worried because my boots had leaked from walking in the rain all day and wet feet were prime territory for blisters. Out of necessity, I hung my socks on the warm radiator behind my chair. I slipped my boots under the heater hoping to dry them for the rest of that day's journey. With my hands wrapped around a hot café con leche,

I put my feet up on the chair across from me and slowly leaned back to rest against the heater, warming my tired body. At home, I would never consider doing something like this at a bar, however since becoming a pilgrim, it seemed I could do nothing wrong.

Although Stefan was only twenty-three years old, almost half my age, his philosophical wisdom and insight were years beyond his age. We shared stories about what we most loved about being on the Camino and how we both delighted in meeting different people of any age or culture. Through this conversation I began to gain a clearer picture of myself. By seeing the simple beauty in people who yearn to give love and be love, I realized I often acted as a mirror reflecting their own beauty onto themselves. I finally admitted to being a hopeless romantic who values the absolute truth over everything else. Stefan said I was "sympatica," a Spanish word that doesn't translate easily but basically describes a funny person who is friendly and open towards people. Someone who inspires others with the freedom to be who they are, without the fear of being judged. I liked being sympatica. Besides I have been called far worse things!

By the time we finished our second café con leche. My socks and boots had finally dried and I was warm again. With a three hour walk ahead of us to the next village, we reluctantly left the comfort of the noisy bar returning to the solitude of the outdoors. Although it was still raining heavily, I had learned to appreciate any kind of weather since it always presented a new experience. I walked, matching Stefan's faster pace, the same way I would follow the stroke if I were rowing in a crew boat. The sound of each footstep was like a mantra taking me deeper into a state of walking meditation. In this state, I was freed of the intense pain from my knee and a pulled Achilles tendon. In time, almost naturally, we separated each preferring to walk alone at our own accustomed pace.

For two hours I trudged along in the rain. Trying desperately to avoid thoughts I did not want to face, I amused myself by following the raindrops as they landed on the tip of my hooded jacket. From there they would drop onto the end of my nose, hanging loosely until the movement of my body forced their release, falling onto the ground and becoming lost in the dirt under my feet. Eventually it eased my mind into a stillness that allowed for deeper awareness and consciousness. By focusing on the raindrops, other noises and distractions were avoided leaving my mind free to meditate in calmness.

My thoughts shifted to an experience a few nights ago when I was at a refugio in a small village. We were informed not to prepare dinner since a group of villagers would be arriving to prepare a traditional three course meal for the pilgrims that night. A lively group of men and women arrived, loaded with grocery bags filled with food. They prepared a delicious meal and served us, refusing to accept any offer of help. During dinner, we somehow communicated without knowledge of our respective languages. I found out that most of the men had walked the Camino numerous times in the past and this was their way of serving the pilgrims.

They presented a bottle of dark red wine and carefully poured it into a glass decanter with a spout. Miguel, one of the village men, in a demonstrative gesture, grabbed the glass decanter and tilted his head back. By pouring the wine onto his forehead, it ran over the bridge of his nose and it flowed directly into his mouth. Everyone cheered in delight and he passed the decanter onto the next person who repeated the ritual. This social style of drinking wine was not unlike the way the raindrops ran along my hood that day.

As I walked, the established discipline of meditation had weakened. Physically, it was becoming impossible to walk because of the excruciating pain in my knee. Being alone in the inclement weather was constantly testing my character and my patience. There was nowhere to stop for a rest so the rain continually poured over me. Finally, I arrived in what appeared to be an old deserted village. It was siesta time so even if someone had lived there, the shutters on the windows were closed and the streets empty. Seeking a reprieve from the incessant rain, I crouched down in the doorway of a building. Because of the size of my backpack, I could not get far enough into the doorway to be sheltered from the rain. I felt exceptionally lonely so I got up and started following the yellow arrows to a road that gently curved down the side of a small hill, pointing to the direction of the ominous Meseta in the distance.

I stopped at the top of the hill to look back at the quaint village that seemed totally surreal to me. I thought about rowing again. A rower has the advantage of being able to see where they have just been. Since they are sitting backwards in the boat, winning a race affords the rower the added gratification of seeing their opponents lose. On the other hand, if they are losing the race, the rower can't see anyone. I have been in both situations and definitely prefer the first one. Standing there for a moment, I began to question where the people were. Did they not see the Canadian peregrina completely drenched walking alone in the unrelenting Spanish rain?

Weren't they worried about me? What did they think of the pilgrims walking through their little village every day, especially the thousands that walk in the summer? Somehow, I felt as though I had been deserted by the Camino.

There were still six kilometers left to walk to the next village that had a refugio, which would take about an hour and a half. Stopping for a water break, I sat down on the side of the road and took out my diary to look at the intentions I had written down. By reviewing my intentions, it was obvious to me a definite pattern was developing. Using the power of the subjective mind, over time I was becoming the intentions that I repeated aloud. This discipline was providing the clarity I needed to build the foundation for my goals to become a reality. With clarity of my vision, I could begin to define my higher purpose.

On arrival at the refugio, I met two Swedish pilgrims and we all registered with the hospitalero. Our credentials were stamped with a "sello" as proof we had walked that day. If we made it to Santiago, the stamps in our credentials would confirm that we walked the pilgrimage route. This permitted us to receive the coveted Compostela; a certificate given to pilgrims who completed at least the last 100 kilometers of the Camino for spiritual or religious reasons.

I took a shower, hung my clothes on the frame of my bed to air out and then found my way to the local bar. I ordered a glass of red wine. My mind wandered trying to make sense of the impressions of that day as I busied myself writing in my journal. Entering the conversation with Stefan in my diary, I considered a new possibility about communication on the Camino. I think pilgrims communicate in their own way through a complex unspoken tongue, understood soul to soul, in an ageless state that is born in the timelessness of the Camino.

When I returned to the refugio, it was too cold to do anything but go to bed. I slept peacefully dreaming that night about when my daughters were young children. Waking up in the morning, I forgot where I was. Disoriented, I bolted upright and frantically scanned the room from the top bunk, looking for my daughters. Once I was outside of my sleeping bag, the air was very cold, bringing an abrupt ending to the dream world. My children were nowhere near.

Following my routine, I methodically packed my things in their allocated space in the backpack to distribute the weight for optimum comfort. It was 26 kilometers to Villafranca del Bierzo, the next destination. I left in the darkness of a Spanish winter morning to walk in peace under the stars of the Milky Way. The first thing I did was pick up a stone for my girls. Putting sorrow into the stone, I carefully placed it down, leaving their sorrow behind. I continued to pick up stones for my sisters, my brother and all of our big Catholic family. Fortunately for me, there was an endless supply to reach for.

I walked about two hours before finally reaching a village. There were a few homes on a main street and gratefully they had a little store that was open. I went inside to find an elderly woman hunched over on a wooden stool behind the counter. "Hola," I said and she grunted back to me. I bought two bananas and a chocolate bar and returned to follow the yellow arrows.

Another hour passed. In the stillness of the morning air, the time quietly slips away with a quickness that appears to have no movement. I stop to rest on the side of the road, to take off my boots and socks to air my feet, re-apply a coat of petroleum jelly and change my socks in an effort to avoid painful blisters. So far this precaution has protected my feet but my twisted ankle is quite swollen, forcing the tips of my toes into the front of my boot, causing me a lot of pain. Even though I'm concerned that removing my boot will only worsen the problem, I decide that blister prevention treatment must prevail. I could always wear lighter socks to compensate for the swelling.

Many thoughts today have to do with money and success in the struggle to balance the simple life of a pilgrim and my world back home in Toronto. The simple needs of a pilgrim life provided a platform for living congruent with my virtues, but the question remained; could these values be transferred home intact?

Four hours later, I arrive in Tosantos with its beautiful Cathedral. To my disappointment it is locked. I found a bar and asked for two café con leche. The first one I drank quickly to warm up. The second I sipped slowly and thoroughly enjoyed. As I shouldered my backpack and walked out of the village I heard a familiar voice calling me. It was Stefan. We walked the rest of the way together arriving at the refugio at two o'clock in the afternoon. This was perfect because I could wash my clothes and have enough time to dry them on the electric heaters before they were turned off at 10:00 p.m.

Deciding to have an afternoon nap, I snuggled into my sleeping bag, snoozing peacefully for about an hour. I woke to the sound of Stefan quietly turning the pages of his Bible. We went to the bar and Stefan suggested I try drinking warm red wine, a customary winter drink his German grandmother used to make. We ate tapas with the warm wine and told more stories of our lives back home.

When we returned to the refugio, three young German pilgrims arrived. One of the girls, Mona, reminded me of my oldest daughter Tara who, at the time, was also 19. I told her everything about my daughters, exuding the sense of pride only a mother can display. As I spoke, I felt the young women wanted to have a closer bond with me. I desperately wanted to care for them as my own children, especially at this time when I missed them so much. Knowing the young women needed to walk on their own journey, I gave them my love. We pooled our food to make chorizo sandwiches and sheep cheese for dinner. With nothing to do in the cold refugio, we returned to the bar.

Talking to the three girls reminded me how much I missed my daughters. Today, I felt completely disconnected from them as though they were far away, but only in the physical realm. This brought back memories of the days they were born, when the doctor cut the umbilical cord. It was a crucial moment of maternal awakening. My role as a mother reached a transitional stage. No longer was I nurturing the needs of the fetus within my womb instead I would nurture the mind, body and soul of my babies in the external world, always mindful of the spiritual realm of their souls as part of the universe. In a similar way, the Camino represented another transitional point in my life. Leaving home I was cut off from the physical world as I knew it. On the Camino, my maternal role was evolving as a peregrina on the path to nurturing universal love.

Suddenly anxious, I went outside to telephone my daughters from a pay phone booth on the deserted street. Tara answered the phone and I was relieved she was home. I could hear the excitement in her voice as I told stories about my experiences. It was difficult to talk about my emotions with her so instead I described the people, the countryside, the food, the customs and the language. She wanted to hear about the other pilgrims and she was particularly interested in hearing about the young student, Stefan from Argentina, whom I kept meeting along the way. I told her that I was leaving stones filled with her sorrow on the Camino. She didn't respond to this, but I know she understood the concept of this ritual. With youthful energy, Tara filled me in on her own new life. She told me all about her school courses and the new friends she had met. Finally, too cold to stand outside any longer we finished our conversation with a tearful "I love you" and a long goodbye.

Even though I was shaking uncontrollably with the cold, I called my middle daughter Meghan and grew upset when she wasn't home. Since she was living with me in Toronto at the time and only 16 years old, I had arranged for a friend to move in with her while I was in Spain. I was concerned about how they were managing in my absence since they had no way of reaching me, if there was an emergency. Disappointed, my only option was to leave a recorded message for her on voice mail. It always seemed that Meghan, as the middle child was short-changed, regardless of how hard I tried to avoid this. I left a long detailed message hoping she would realize how much I loved her.

Then I called my youngest daughter Simone. At the age of 14 her unlimited energy and excitement came through over the phone. She was thrilled to hear from me and raced on about a new friend at school who snorts when she laughs, reminding her of me. We laughed together (I snorted as well) and I warned her that even though she did not live with me anymore, I would show up in other people and different places in her life. With her casual youthful attitude she said, "Whatever." How I missed the fast teen talk and the lingo that had become so familiar to me. Simone expressed her worry about me walking alone. I told her not to worry because the Spanish people were very helpful and friendly to the winter pilgrims especially. "Love ya," I said quickly before my emotions would take over my ability to talk. Simone said she loved me and gave me a kiss before saying her final goodbye.

Surprisingly, the telephone calls made me miss my daughters even more, longing for their physical presence. After I hung up the phone I thought about what they were going through at home while I was walking the Camino. They were on a pilgrimage as well, each on their own journey to find the way that best suited them.

On my way back inside the refugio I took stock of my progress. If I were to divide this journey into the four stages of a rowing race; the start, the middle, the wall and the finish, on the Camino I had just reached the middle. Here rowers must maintain consistency even as their bodies scream to stop. Just like tackling the Meseta, the rowing race is won in the mind of the athlete. The middle is the longest section of the race, covering almost half the entire distance. My coach insisted that the race begins at the halfway point. His theory postulated that everything up to the halfway point, was in preparation for the real race. If he is right, that means on this journey, I'm halfway into it. In other words, the race is just beginning.

First I would have to face the potential Meseta madness that legend has it, can completely overwhelm a pilgrim.

10

meseta madness

*T*he walk into Burgos the day before ended with a grueling eight kilometer tramp through a dreary industrial park land that held no appeal for a pilgrim like me. The Camino had exposed me to the beauty of nature leaving me uninterested in the confines of the big city. Burgos is closely linked to the famous El Cid, who fought the Moors to regain the region of Castile in the 15th century. Stefan, the Argentinean, had walked into the city with me providing some relief from the boredom passing faded factories until we reached the old quarter. Following the yellow arrows, we were led to a refugio set deep within a forested park. The sign on the door directed us to pick up the key at a house close by. No one was home so we hid our backpacks behind the building and left to discover the old city.

This was a dramatic city filled with artistic historical monuments. We stumbled upon the remains of a castle from the 9th century with a wide stone staircase hugging a crumbling wall. We chased each other up and down the stairs with youthful laughter, challenging our recently acquired mountain climbing skills. When we stopped to rest, I raised my hand and placed my palm against the cold stone wall with the gentleness one would caress a new born baby. Touching it ever so lightly, I could feel the ancient history of the stones, wondering if other pilgrims had done the same thing before me. I questioned who the masons were who put these stones in place centuries ago. Each day as I had carried sorrow stones, my purpose became more clear to me. Did the masons who brought their skills to this site also find purpose working with the stone?

Entering the doorway of the Gothic church of Iglesia San Nicolas, we found a peaceful place resting in the spiritual embrace of the Camino. As much as the architectural marvels in Burgos fascinated me, as a simple pilgrim I was desperate to get back to walking in the openness of the natural Spanish terrain.

The next morning came quickly. Characteristically, I woke before anyone else, packed my things and left. It was 6:30 a.m. and the rain started as soon as I stepped outside. A thin layer of frost carpeted the streets, left from last night's freezing rain. My walking poles offered little support on the slippery surface. Purposely I wanted to be out of my comfort zone, to practise facing my fear. There was a sense of security in putting one foot in front of the other for the sheer reason I was moving forward.

I was nervous today about finding my way through the labyrinth of this large city. It was difficult to locate the arrows painted on the pavement and buildings because they were not always positioned at eye level. In the darkness before dawn, I made my way cautiously relying heavily on my intuition. I could see tiny streams of light cast on the wall of a building showing the familiar scallop shell to assure me I was going in the right direction out of the city. As I walked, the task of following yellow arrows to find the way struck me as a metaphor for life. The yellow arrows represent signs that appear to us occasionally, perhaps as coincidences or a sense of deja vu, telling us we are going in the right direction. Living in Toronto I was easily distracted, believing that if I reached certain material goals, then I was on the right path in my personal and business life. Now I was beginning to consider the possibility that I had missed a few arrows along the way and maybe I had been lost.

While doing research about the Camino, I read that on the Meseta one can completely lose their mind. This 200 kilometer section is relatively flat, barren and entirely open to the elements. It's like walking through the mammoth wheat fields of Saskatchewan or the vast flatness of Kansas, with the golden horizon and blue sky stretching on forever. The Meseta is a completely different experience for summer pilgrims when there could be as many as 1000 people a day walking the path, battling the heat of the blazing sun beating on their backs.

The pilgrim guide suggested I buy food and supplies in Burgos because it would be a 23 km walk through the Meseta to get to Hontanas, the next village with a store. I stopped to buy yogurt, fruit and some chocolate covered digestive cookies which had become a special treat I enjoyed at the end of the day. Confident I had everything I needed for this journey, I closed my backpack and started walking. The warmth of the morning sun rising behind me, showered rays of light around the entire landscape in the shape of a scallop shell. Turning around, I basked in the warmth of the sunrise breaking the horizon with the light of a glorious new day.

As usual, I spent the first hour of my walk focusing on

self-love. I opened my body and heart to the possibility of receiving love. I walked with my shoulders pulled back, standing tall, smiling inwardly as I discovered this joyful expression within my being. I tried to imagine what it would be like to really love myself. On the Meseta my mind wandered to places I had not been to in a long time. I thought about my daughters again, repeating the intention to always be a loving mother. I thought if I could love myself as much as I love my daughters, that would give me something to aspire to. I wondered what they were doing at that very moment in time.

Many hours passed. At first it was cold with light snow falling that eventually changed to freezing rain. My patience was thinning and I was annoyed at the prospect of being tested yet again. Continuing to put one foot in front of the other, there was no shelter from the pervasive disquiet of the Meseta. Finding a small rock, I sat down to rest, reaching into my backpack for water and something to eat. My knee was aching. At this rate I felt that even if I did make it to the end of the Camino, all I would have to show for my efforts would be a catalogue of sundry stories about my injuries.

By early afternoon, I still had not seen anyone since I left that morning and I was becoming convinced that I was going the wrong way. After completing at least three more kilometers without seeing one yellow arrow, I repeatedly asked for some kind of a sign or omen, but this time nothing appeared.

Could this be an early onset of Meseta madness?

Thinking a different perspective might help, I turned around and looked back the way I came. Immediately my eyes were drawn to a grouping of stones on the path. Looking more closely I could see they were placed in the shape of an arrow and it was pointing toward me. I smiled, relieved there was a sign after all. The direction of the stone arrow confirmed I was walking the right way. With humble gratitude I thanked the considerate pilgrim who went before me and placed that stone arrow, assuming the pilgrim had experienced the same doubts. Through this I learned, if you ask for a sign, one will be delivered.

The view in front of me remained unchanged for hours. Flat, barren, unyielding and lonely. It was as though I was laboring on a treadmill to nowhere. Walking past wheat field after wheat field, I soon arrived in a small village boasting a local church with a bell tower. On my journey, I had made a point of entering the churches and cathedrals along the Camino to study the statues and paintings of saints. Curious, I entered the little church. When I looked into the eyes of the saints, it appeared as though they could see something in the mirror of the universe, I could not. The artisans had depicted vision and passion through their eyes. The Saints were looking far beyond this world towards their life purpose. It seemed to me they were facing their fear. Once again, I was reminded of Dino's interpretation of a saint represented as someone who faces their fear.

I left 200 pesetas in the donation box at the back of the church. Lighting a candle, I said a prayer for my dear mother who had given so much of herself to me. Outside the church I stooped to pick up a stone for her. I carried this one for an especially long time before eventually placing it down.

The path to Hontanas was a wide dirt road with tractor tracks cast in the mud, cutting deeply down the middle. It rained relentlessly, soaking me through to the skin and turning the path into a sea of mud. I struggled to walk as the thick, heavy clumps stuck like glue to the sides and bottom of my hiking boots, resisting the upward pull of my leg. Wet sucking noises were released each time the air raced into the vacuum created as I hauled my boot out of the deep mud. The added weight aggravated my frustrations, slowing my pace. My body was sore, my mind intolerant. I was cold, hungry and tired. I just wanted to get to the refugio or go home to the comfort of my fresh, clean-sheeted bed. I couldn't see the town that was supposed to be less than a kilometer ahead. The sun was setting swiftly and I was running out of daylight. I could feel the chill of the oncoming night cooling my already quivering, damp body. Where was Hontanas?

The repetitive sucking sound made each time I tugged my boot from the mud, triggered and brought to the surface emotions I had been burying all my life. Now they were exposed and I became terribly vulnerable to despair and discouragement. Since I was too tired to understand what was happening, my rising anger became a purgative for my frustrations. Looking for any kind of relief from the annoying sound and the added weight of the wet mud clinging onto my boots, I decided to try walking on the shoulder of the road. With my first step I sunk into a gooey morass up to my knee. The mud seeped inside my boots and I swore out loud. I was irritated by this stupid, ridiculously slapstick part of the journey. I was incensed at the Camino because it was drawing out an aspect of my personality I did not like.

The voices in my mind started to take control urging me to just call this the finish line and quit. I could stop walking at anytime and find a bus to take me to the end of the Meseta. What was I trying to prove to myself? That I was unstoppable?

Should I go back home and hide behind some other identity? Maybe get a new corporate job or do something familiar from the world of the old Sue Kenney.

Fear. Fear. Fear. It was taking over my thinking and paralyzing my life and actions. I started blaming other people and situations for everything. I hated this day. I hated the Meseta. Where was Stefan now when I really needed someone to talk to? I had asked for a sign, where was it? I felt deserted, miserable and forsaken. Now I knew why so many pilgrims took a bus through this hell. I had even stopped my selfless ritual of picking up sorrow stones. I had no physical or emotional strength left to carry even a random thought. I was numb in my body, mind and spirit.

A fast walking Swiss pilgrim approached from behind. I asked him if he knew where the next village was located. "About 500 meters ahead." he said. Looking forward, I could see nothing except flat land. I wondered to myself if he knew what he was talking about. Oblivious to my internal turmoil he talked endlessly asking me questions I did not feel like answering. Questions about where I was from and why I was walking the Camino. I had no patience left. My mind was dead and I couldn't think about how to answer any questions. With all the passion drained from my heart, I told him I couldn't talk right now. Besides, his walking pace was far too fast for my sore knee and I couldn't keep up with him. He quickly walked on.

In the distance a huge black circle punctuated the darkened fields. I watched as the speedy pilgrim faded into its blackness. Poised below the surface, it appeared as a depression in the earth. Like a scene in a horror movie, the blackness creeping forward suddenly opened beneath me and revealed through the foggy mist, the old city of Hontanas in its glorious, shimmering wetness.

I took a deep breath, lifted my head to look forward and once again opened myself to surrender to the love of the universe. My awareness blossomed and I could begin to feel a graceful energy surge throughout me. By discerning fear as a concern, I let it go. I became more aware of my capacity for this universal love and I was truly grateful.

One can lose their mind on the Meseta. On this part of the journey, I had lost my mind yet ironically on the Meseta I was beginning to find it again, I was unaware that when I would look back on its torment from a distance, it would appear as a mirage.

11

hell in hontanas

*T*he road sloped downward into the belly of an ancient village. The rain stopped and the thick heavy mud transformed into a slippery stone road leading to the historic village, complete with a 14th century church bell tower, rising to meet the heavenly sky.

It was dark now and with today's Meseta's madness behind me, my pace quickened in anticipation of a well-earned rest. I caught up to Stefan and two other pilgrims walking through the dark empty streets and we searched for a place to sleep that night. Outside the doorway of an old decaying building stood a short, balding Spaniard wearing an old plaid shirt that was far too small to cover his protruding belly. Seeing us he smiled a devilish grin and opened the door to his bar tempting us with the comforts of warmth and shelter. Along the Camino, I'd heard about a certain creepy character with a hostel and bar in this town whose notoriety preceded him. Was this the place? Our pilgrim guide stated that all the other refugios in Hontanas were closed in the winter, leaving me very concerned that this could be our only option for that night. Leery but desperate for any relief from the mud and rain, we entered.

Inside, the room was dark with the smell of stale beer and dampness in the air. Laundry hung across a rope hanging over the tables of the dining room, displaying a line of worn out men's white briefs. At the back of the main floor, he sold supplies and food. I selected a container of yogurt from the old refrigerator and took it to the front counter to pay. Taking the money from my hand, he paused staring at me with a disgusting smirk and a look in his eyes like a man who had been denied the pleasures of a woman for a long, long time. Repelled by his actions, I turned away.

Uncomfortable with the surroundings and its proprietor, I turned to walk out the door. Stefan pointed out an Espresso machine behind the counter and asked for a café con leche. Glaring at Stefan in a loud, forceful voice the man insisted he would only make coffee if we agreed to stay the night at his hostel. I could see that Stefan was angered by the tone of the conversation. Together we decided we would rather walk to the next village in the dark than stay in this hellish place.

Once outside, we didn't know where to go but at least we were content to be walking with the safety of the Camino below our feet. To our surprise and relief, not far down the road we came upon another hostel whose open door welcomed us. How soon my gratitude returned! Inside the refugio we removed our muddy boots and right away the coldness of the building became apparent. Back at home, I would have complained to someone about this but now I was a pilgrim, content to have a warm sleeping bag, a bunk-bed and the company of other pilgrims under a roof.

Downstairs, in the clean and simple kitchen, two pilgrims, an American and a French woman were sitting at an old wooden table. They told me what I could already feel that there was no heat in the building. We boiled water for tea and talked until our bodies started shivering uncontrollably in the cold damp room. Without warning, the kitchen door flew open and the three young German girls, who reminded me of my daughters, entered. What a wonderful surprise! It was after 8 p.m. and they looked like they had been to hell and back again. Dirt and mud was caked all over their clothes and boots. I ran over and hugged each of them. Mona thanked me for the birthday postcard and the chocolate bar I had left for her at the refugio yesterday. They talked excitedly about their experiences during the last kilometer to Hontanas. Unable to see anything in the dark, they had to get down on their hands and knees to feel their way along the path. Virtually crawling into the village, the same creepy hospitalero tried to persuade them to stay at his hostel. They too immediately recognized his devilish nature and refused his invitation.

That night at the refugio there was nothing to do and nowhere to go, since everything was closed for the winter. All went to bed early. My body and mind were weary and I fell asleep, easily slipping into the familiar comfort of my own pilgrim heart.

12

finding bernie

*M*y sleeping bag was pulled tightly up over my head. My neck was stretched so that my mouth could reach the opening of the metal zipper, allowing me to breathe in the fresh cold winter air. Sleeping in a strange place every night was one adjustment to contend with, but worse than that, I hated stepping out of my warm sleeping bag in the morning only to be greeted by the ice cold floor. To save carrying extra weight, I hadn't packed pajamas, opting instead to sleep in my black sport underwear and a sleeveless vest. The idea of having to completely strip down in the cold was out of the question, so they also doubled as a first layer of clothing during the day.

I left the refugio in Hontanas early that morning, anxious to be walking during that majestic time of day when the last moments of darkness rested on the Meseta. I had grown accustomed to anticipating the beauty and peace I experienced just before the sun found its way over the horizon. On this day however, I would have gladly missed it. Today I felt lonely. Fortunately, the established rituals had become routine, leaving me no choice about whether to walk or not. I was still a pilgrim with at least a few more days of solitary walking on the Meseta before I would reach my much anticipated heavenly mountains of Cebreiro.

As I walked, my mind eased into a calm, meditative state. For the first five kilometers that day, I focused on my intention of being a more loving parent. I approached the ruins of the Convent of San Anton that dates back to the 12th century, where the resident monks cared for pilgrims who suffered from *San Anton's Fire* a horrible leprosy-like disease. I tried to imagine what it would have been like for those long-ago pilgrims, who were true saints facing not only their personal fears, but physical mortification and death itself. My worst discomfort was insignificant in comparison.

The land around me was flat and desolate, filled with wheat fields laying dormant in anticipation of Spring. After two hours of walking I had covered 10 kilometers and I arrived at the next village tired and hungry. Nestled around the side of the mountain and built in cascading layers, was the village of Castrojeriz. An air of mystery surrounded its ancient architecture. Perched high on top of a small mountain that juts out of the flatland, is a Roman ruin, allegedly built by Julius Ceasar. As I neared the village, the Camino path had changed from hardened dirt on wide open flat land, to cobblestone laid by hand centuries ago.

It was time for a warm cup of café con leche. I walked a short distance through the sleepy village, and stopped at the first local bar I came to called La Taberna. Turning the handle, I opened the door and suddenly a large German Shepherd dog darted across the room towards me. Just as he started to jump up on me, a man behind the counter (who was presumably the dog's owner) called out in Spanish and fortunately for me the dog responded immediately. In appreciation, I let out a big sigh of relief.

I looked around the room to see that all the tables were empty and I was the only one present. Being alone was becoming the norm for me. I picked out a table that gave me a full view of the front door. Sliding my backpack from my shoulders, the weight of it made a loud thud as it dropped to the floor. Sitting down, I took off my boots and then walked up to the counter admiring the home-made empanada displayed. Following a brief conversation with the owner, who spoke only Spanish, I decided to order a café con leche and some tostada (toast). Returning to the table, I put both my feet on the chair across from me and waited patiently for my order to arrive.

I discovered an internet station in the corner of the room reminding me that I should access my e-mail. Since leaving Toronto, I hadn't been able to get on-line for many reasons; locations were closed, the computers broken, systems were down or I simply didn't have time to stop and write. I thought I would check my email but for some reason, I couldn't get access to the server. I had absolutely no interest in trying to wrestle with technology while on a spiritual quest, instead just accepting that I wouldn't be communicating with anyone on-line.

I had refused to bring my cell phone with me even though everyone I spoke to thought I should have it just in case. I was a single woman walking alone in a foreign country and it was expected that I would rely on modern technology for my safety. To me, a cell phone gave only a false sense of security. So much of my life at home had been centered around planning for just-in-case situations like portable generators, home alarm systems, micro-chip implants in dogs and a spare tire in my trunk. In 24 years of driving, I used my spare tire once and even then it was a driver mechanic who came to my rescue. I am sure if I had needed a tire, he would have gladly obliged. On the Camino, I wanted to shed the need to plan for every possible scenario and instead be able to live in the moment. My backup plan consisted of relying on the universe and the good intentions of strangers in a time of need. More importantly, I wanted to have the opportunity to help others, too.

The man brought me thick white toast and freshly brewed coffee. Its aroma was a welcome familiarity. He told me the dog's name was Bernie. Since my middle name is Bernadette I felt a kindred spirit towards this special animal. Bernie had found a place to sleep under the table, resting against my legs, he laid on top of my boots. Out of nowhere, a little bird came flying over to my table and perched itself on the edge of my plate. Confidently, without any concern for my presence, it started to peck at my toast. Leaning back in my chair, I smiled with interest and looked around for the owner, who was nowhere in sight. I laughed, startling the bird and it flew to an open cage I hadn't noticed on the other side room. There weren't many birds on the Camino but there was no shortage of avian entertainment in this restaurant.

Bernie was comfortably sleeping at my feet, giving me the feeling I was a special guest. His unconditional love reminded me how much I missed our family dog, Ranger, who lived for our attention and love. After walking all morning alone, I welcomed his companionship. Leaning down, I scratched him behind the ears and he stretched his neck. Bernie knew how to get what he wanted out of life.

Just as I was prepared to leave, my pilgrim friend, Stefan the young Argentinean, arrived. Feeling lonely that day I decided to stay longer. He ordered breakfast and we were soon talking like two old friends sharing life stories. Stefan updated me about some of the other pilgrims on the Camino. I found out that Karl the German, had some troubles with his knee and had to stay back and rest. Apparently, Dino was still walking barefoot and he was a few days behind us. When I first met Dino I remember him saying he wasn't sure that he would walk the entire route to Santiago. That struck me as unusual, since I had it in my mind from the very beginning, that I was not going to stop until I made it to Santiago.

Stefan and I left the bar and Bernie followed us. His owners didn't object to him leaving so I assumed he would escort us to the outskirts and then return home. At the edge of the village we stopped to say goodbye to our new friend but it seemed Bernie had his own idea. We encouraged him to go back (Stefan spoke imploringly in Spanish) but Bernie ignored our pleading. He wasn't going anywhere without us and continued to walk ahead, confidently showing the way.

The hours slipped by and it was a beautiful sunny day on the Meseta. You could see across the flat landscape for many miles. Stefan was quite concerned that Bernie was still with us and he asked me what I thought we should do. I said, "Don't worry, Bernie is a pilgrim dog. He knows where he is going and can find his way home too. I'm sure of it." Somehow I knew that Bernie was supposed to be there with us, I just didn't know why. Perhaps I had something to learn from him.

Stefan and I often walked apart from each other as it was sometimes my preference to walk alone. Bernie was a smart dog and would run from Stefan, then back to me, spending equal time with each of us. If he saw that we were going in the wrong direction, he would redirect us onto the right path. Occasionally, we would come across other dogs who were fenced-in or tied up for safety. Bernie appeared to know all the dogs and he proudly positioned himself just out of their reach, teasing them with his Camino freedom. I imagined he was actually telling the dogs about the wonders of being a pilgrim. It occurred to me that I was like Bernie. I would take my discoveries on the Camino world back home to share with people who wouldn't have the opportunity to experience this type of a journey themselves.

Walking with Bernie that day I felt safe from danger, assured my new friend would protect me in any situation. Occasionally I would stop to rest sitting down on the side of the road. During these rest periods Bernie always stayed close to me. Maybe it was because he loved Spanish cheese as much as I did!

One of my daily rituals on the Camino was to spend time watching the sun rise and set. In the morning, I usually started to walk in the dark. Since I was walking from east to west, as the sun rose its warmth would cover my back. Often I stopped to turn around and admire the sun showing itself on the horizon.

One time in a refugio I saw a written sign in English that said, "A pilgrim must always say thank you." I was so grateful for all of my experiences on the Camino that I longed to acknowledge that gratitude. At the end of each day, I would walk the last kilometer, conscious of all the things I was grateful for that day.

When my daughters were young we had a bedtime ritual.

I would read a story or sometimes we would tell stories to each other, followed by a prayer. Then, I would tuck them into bed, one at a time asking them to remember someone or something that felt good that day encouraging them to express their gratitude. This was my way of teaching them the importance of respect for people and the value of being grateful. We often forget what people do to us and we sometimes forget what people say to us, but we never forget how they make us feel. Thank you Bernie!

That day I was grateful for the sun, for the clouds, for the moon, for the stars, for the earth and for the Camino. It was as though it was the first time I could see the natural beauty in everything around me. There was a new sense of joy that I believe was the result of being in a state of gratitude every day. Had I discovered one of life's mysteries? Was it hidden from my view by the veil of familiarity? By leaving familiarity behind, the simple life of a pilgrim showed me the way to a new level of awareness.

Thirty-four kilometers later, we three arrived in the village of Fromista. Stefan went ahead to locate the refugio. I stopped to watch the glowing sunset with Bernie sitting at my feet. This was a very special moment as I stood there in silence honoring the end of another Camino day. There were voices in the background that I tried to ignore, from people trying to get our attention. "Hola! Hola, Bernie!" I turned toward them and saw a group of young kids excitedly calling out and waving to Bernie. Although, it was obvious that he loved all the attention, he stayed there with me. I smiled to the local villagers and laughed inwardly in admiration of Bernie's world. I waved goodbye and we left in search of the way to the refugio.

Minutes later, Bernie and I arrived at a beautiful old building with big doors leading into a foyer. As soon as I opened the door, Bernie ran into the room and the hospitalera jumped up from behind her desk and started yelling at him in Spanish, calling him by name. Stefan appeared just as she was chasing Bernie out the front door. Stefan then told me that he had heard about my four-legged friend from the people at the refugio. "Bernie is the legendary dog of the Camino," he said. "Each morning, Bernie chooses one or two pilgrims to walk with. Today, we were the chosen pilgrims. Once he arrives in Fromista, 24 kilometers from his home, he refuses to walk back home again. Therefore, someone from the village has to drive him all the way back to Castrojeriz or call his owners who then have to come and pick him up." We both laughed at Bernie's ways, knowing in our hearts that we were truly honored to have experienced a day with one of the greatest legends of the Camino de Santiago.

My journey walking with Bernie that day taught me valuable life lessons. I believe he was sent to guide me as an example of how to surrender to the goodwill of others, without any expectation, he trusted the Camino. He walked as a free spirit, confident he would always find his way home. He loved the outdoors and never rushed his journey. He communicated with everyone, expecting nothing in return. He chose whom he would walk with on the Camino and I was honored to be one of the chosen few. Bernie allowed his love to flow freely without any conditions – except for a car ride back home.

The art of walking every day had the pleasing effect of clearing my mind and awakening my body with a familiar rhythm I had come to love. The passing scenery was experienced in a heightened state of awareness, with all of my senses engaged; my eyes captured the pictures, my nose breathed in the aroma of the village, my ears listened to the music of the language, my mouth savored the full-flavored Camino air, while my feet touched the earth walked by millions of pilgrims before me. My personal awakening was becoming more apparent with each day that passed.

13

reflecting on bodhichitta

On the beaches of Fisterre, it is customary for pilgrims to pick up a scallop shell to bring home as proof of their journey. The origin of this custom is obscure, but one possible explanation may be found in the romantic tale of a knight who was traveling alone by horse to Santiago, from Mont Saint Michel, France. The knight was riding along the shore when he and his horse were dragged out to sea by the strong incoming tide. He prayed for St. James to come to his rescue. Magically, a bridge of white scallop shells rose out of the water allowing the knight to ride safely back to shore; hence the significance of the scallop shell. Personally, I wasn't that interested in finding a shell to bring home from the Camino because I had discovered my own comfort in the stones I found and carried along the way.

Mont Saint Michel is the site of a Gothic Abbey constructed in the 8th century by people who carried tons of stone by hand. They brought the stones from Brittany and hauled them up the 265-foot peak. The village now rises up from the sea, which comes pounding in at high tide, creating an island. It has become a pilgrimage destination in its own rite.

With only 200 kilometers left of my journey to Santiago, I was again feeling the parachutist's sense of ground rush. Instead of me heading towards the end of the Camino, it seemed to be rushing uncontrollably towards me. Walking into the city of Leon I struggled at first to find the yellow arrows. Instead there were brass scallop shells imbedded in the pavement of the roads and walls of buildings to help lead the pilgrims through the ancient city. This was once a Roman garrison town where in the early 16th century the Knights of Santiago allegedly met in what is now a five star Parador hotel. I arrived in Leon to find the Convento Santa Maria de las Carbajalas, (the convent of the Madres Benedictinas) where I would be staying that night.

A cheerful hospitalero greeted me speaking Spanish. He welcomed me to the convent and proceeded to notify me of the rules. Of course I didn't understand anything except the curfew time of 10:00 p.m. and that was only because it was listed on a sign, hanging on the wall. After registering, I went upstairs to find a clean and simple bunkroom. I selected a top bunk in the middle of the large room and claimed my home for the evening. Of the few pilgrims who were there, Astrid, the Swiss pilgrim I met earlier that day, was the only person I recognized. She informed me there would be a pilgrim blessing at 9:00 p.m. After the moving experience in Roncesvalles, I knew without a doubt, I would be there.

Leaving my backpack behind, I grabbed my money pouch and passport and headed to the Plaza Major. This street boasted more of the fine architecture I had admired on my way into the city. As I was looking up in awe of the great gothic cathedral, a woman standing next to me began speaking.

In broken English, she indicated details of the Mother and Child carvings on the facade. Then she pointed to the corners of the building where the Green Man, a pagan figure that is seen on buildings all over the world, was hiding. Without prompting, she informed me there were 125 stained glass windows and 57 roundels in the church. I turned to thank the woman but she was gone. Drawn by its beauty, I walked into the church and stood there, bathed in the magnificence of the illuminated glass. I was grateful once again. This time to the total stranger who drew my attention to this fantastic work of art and devotion. On the Camino, each person I meet adds to the person I am.

Stunned by its beauty, I walked back to the plaza and found Stefan waiting. We went to the Café Europa to catch up on the events of the day over a café con leche. The conversation shifted to a more serious tone as Stefan spoke openly about his parents and the heartbreak they endured because of his rebellious activities as a youth. Along the Camino, he had been reflecting on the causes of his own unhappiness and felt drawn to talk with me about it. I related how I had learned to parent through trial and error. Of course, I had read books and magazines and talked to other parents, but in the end I told him, my parenting skills had developed through real life practical situations.

Stefan spoke with emotion and tears began to fill his eyes. He was saddened by the trouble he had brought to his family. He turned his face away saying he didn't want to make anyone else suffer. I touched his hand waiting for him to speak. I felt my heart ache with his sadness, as though it were my own personal emotion. Unbeknownst to him, I had already left many stones on the path for Stefan, unaware of the true depth of his sorrow.

Now I began to share a level of compassion manifested from within my soul that I didn't know was possible. There is an energy source in the body known as the heart above the heart, where it is said all universal complex communication takes place. Beyond the ability of words, I connected with Stefan from a place in the depths of my deepest compassion, as though I was crying his tears.

The emotion of our conversation had mutually drained our energy. Leaving the café, we hugged and went our separate ways in silence. I walked aimlessly around Leon trying to distill the effects of the experience. By striving for enlightenment on this journey, my ultimate wish was to help others, to free their pain. Was it possible that I was truly having a love affair with myself after all? Had a transformation taken place? Through the discipline of leaving my sorrow on the Camino, had the foundation of self-love increased my level of compassion? Had my ability to feel the magnitude of this compassion reached an altruistic state?

In the Dalai Lama's teachings, I studied that one's wish to achieve enlightenment, together with an altruistic intention to free others from suffering, would create the state of *Bodhichitta*, the highest form of spiritual practice. I wondered, did my desire to discover self-love to live from a place of love, for the benefit of others, represent an altruistic aspect? The final question I asked was if enlightenment would come in the form of a miracle on Cebreiro or was it something else, like a gradually sustaining development grounded in my daily rituals. I asked these questions, putting them out into the universe, without any concerns about where and when I would have an answer. I simply knew it would come.

Walking around the city, I ran into Astrid. She was impatient with my slow pace as I limped along with a stiff knee. She gave the impression of being a woman on a mission to complete her journey within a certain time, regardless of the experiences she might miss. As we walked, she prattled endlessly about the annoying verbose character of an Italian pilgrim she had walked with a few days ago. Half-listening to her, I reflected on the idea that we are mirrors of each other; the faults and qualities seen in others, could be the faults and qualities we see in ourselves.

On the Camino, it is customary to openly greet people you meet along the way. Usually I just said, "Hola" since my Spanish vocabulary was limited. Often the local villagers would respond with "Buen Camino" or they would call out the ancient pilgrim salute, *Ultreya*, meaning "Onward." As a naturally social individual, I loved to get a reaction from strangers with a smile and a greeting. I found myself repeating Hola over and over again because we were now in a city with people everywhere. Exasperated, Astrid turned to me and said, "When there are so many people in the city it's not necessary for you to say hello to everyone."

I asked, "Why not? I love greeting the people and the city people seem enchanted by the pilgrims, marveling in the novelty of it all." She turned and walked over to lean up against a wall, waiting impatiently for me to finish my shopping. I started rummaging through the piles of mittens to find a replacement pair for the one's I had lost, since I would need them heading into the mountains.

As though I was silently called, I looked up from the table to see this woman, likely of Basque heritage, wearing mournful black clothing. She stood out from the crowd. I smiled and greeted her not really aware that she had been sitting in a wheelchair. She wasn't handicapped, perhaps just weakened in some way. Taking both of her hands she cupped the cheeks of my face gently. With a smile that exuded the warmth of a mother's love, she softly whispered, "Ah, peregrina." Then she drew me toward her kissing me three times on each cheek, going back and forth from side to side, as her hold on my face became tighter. It reminded me of the Italian parents of my childhood friends who always squeezed or pinched my cheeks. Instead of resisting a kiss from a stranger, I accepted her love. "Gracias," I said with a wide smile brimming from ear to ear. I turned see to if Astrid had witnessed this wondrous encounter. She had, but just pointed repeatedly to the face of her watch to remind me time was passing and she wanted to leave. So we left, returning to the convent since it was almost time for the pilgrim blessing.

Astrid went back to the bunkroom and I sat on the wooden bench outside the chapel waiting for the others to arrive. My eyes became heavy and I slipped into a peaceful sleep. I woke up as the pilgrims arrived. The excited hospitalero made an entrance; talking continuously in a hushed voice he organized all ten of us on the bench outside the chapel in anticipation for the arrival of the Mother Superior. By his actions, I felt as if I was partaking in a formal religious cere-mony, like my First Communion. The gregarious hospitalero loved talking to people and he took this opportunity to share his words of wisdom about the pilgrimage. Since he only spoke

Spanish, I couldn't understand his message even though he generously directed most of his conversation at me. I did understand his passion and listened intently to the music of his enraptured voice. He spoke nonstop until the Mother Superior was ready to receive us and then he led us into the chapel.

We pilgrims walked up the aisle in single file until the hospitalero divided us evenly to either side of the pews in the front row. I was sent to the right side with Astrid and a Spanish pilgrim, Jose, whom I'd met earlier in a bar that day. We waited in silence.

Respectfully we all stood as the Mother Superior and the nuns entered. The Mother Superior graciously stepped forward to address the group in Spanish with a voice so soft that it forced complete attentiveness. Even though I didn't understand a single phrase, I continued to remain open to her words. It was a short service followed by a casual talk from the Mother Superior. By their smiles of acknowledgment, I could see that the other pilgrims were enchanted by the sincerity of her message.

Walking out of the chapel I waited for Astrid, anxious to ask her to translate what was said during the blessing. In a whispered voice Astrid recounted the words of the Mother Superior who said she had a special message for the pilgrims who were present. She reminded us that everyone has a light within them. As pilgrims, once we have completed the journey to Santiago, our light will be brighter than others. She added, that it was our responsibility to share the light. When we go home, people will want us to go back to being the person we were before walking the Camino. They will resist the changes we went through and we will be tested again and again. Astrid said the Mother Superior assured us this could be overcome. When Astrid was done, I restrained my first reaction to make a value judgment about this message but instead I accepted to consider it as a possibility.

Then Astrid offered to translate the words of the hospitalero. Speaking in perfect English she said that he reminded us we are pilgrims and it's our responsibility to look after each other. He said we should never walk past a pilgrim in need. The pilgrims of the past often walked this journey to obtain a pardon from God or to receive absolution from eternal damnation. In the folklore of the Camino, it is said that if one abandons or disregards a pilgrim in need, no plenary indulgences would be extended. Instead the pilgrim would be obliged to walk their pilgrimage from the very beginning, again. If we walked past a pilgrim in need in this life, would we have to return in another life, to learn the lesson all over again? I wondered if that lesson translated to our daily lives. How many times have I had to learn the same lesson in my life over and over again. If we consciously ignore something that needs our attention, how many times do we suffer the consequences for it?

The next day I started walking in the morning with Astrid. I found the ongoing conversation distracted me from the rituals I had been practicing. Once out of the city we agreed to separate and meet in Mazarife for lunch, since it was only nine kilometers away. However, my injured knee had flared up making it extremely difficult to walk. As a way to deal with the excruciating pain, I started counting my steps again. This reminded me of rowing since I was notorious for counting my strokes out loud. I thought about the time when

I asked my coach Peter how long it would take to become a national level rower. His answer was that it would take a million strokes or about three years of intensive training. Interestingly enough, I went to the world masters race four years after I began intensive training, having completed at least a million rowing strokes. Then I found out that someone had actually counted that it took a million steps to get from St. Jean Pied de Port to Santiago. Based on this, I surmised it would take a million steps for me to become a pilgrim.

No longer able to bend my left knee, I walked slowly towards the bar in Mazarife. Astrid was standing outside on the step with her hands on her hips looking rather annoyed. She had arrived 45 minutes ago and was intent on getting to the next village before the store closed for siesta. She hadn't left, feeling obliged to wait for me. I apologized for the delay and suggested she go ahead since my knee injury was becoming a problem. Without hesitation, she left right away.

I entered the bar setting my backpack down on the floor and ordered a café con leche. As the only one there, I took the liberty of taking my boots off and put my feet up on a chair to alleviate some of the pain. Even boring myself with my loneliness, I left as soon as I finished my drink. Once outside I began the search to find the village refugio. Following the arrows I was directed to an old wooden door. Turning the handle, it swung open to present a disgusting site. Old mattresses were strewn across the floor. In the kitchen a can of beans had been opened and had gone moldy. Dirty dishes filled the sink and there was no heat. I didn't want to stay there but my guidebook showed it was 15 kilometers to the next village. Could I walk that far with my knee injury? I stood there for a long time, weighing my options. I knew I definitely didn't want to sleep or eat at this refugio, so I went outside. Before I knew it, I was walking again following yellow arrows back onto the path that left the city. It appeared the Camino had its own plans for me.

It was now 2:30 p.m. and the sun would set in three hours. To get through the next five hours of walking, burdened with an injury, I called on every skill I had learned in my life and on the Camino so far. The standard distance for a head race in rowing is five kilometers, so I multiplied that distance by three, to cover 15 kilometers. Just as in a rowing race, I knew that I would "hit the wall" at some point within each section. To make it through the wall, I counted to 100 steps and then began counting all over again. This developed into a mantra allowing me to stay focused on my destination.

Passing numerous fallow fields, I took Dino's advice and walked most of the distance on the rough shoulders of the path, so that walking on the uneven ground made use of the smaller muscles in my legs. Eventually I moved to meditating on a point of reference in the space ahead of me concentrating on a maternal style of breathing, something I had learned 18 years ago at Lamaze classes for natural childbirth. I had the feeling that completing the Camino was going to be something like bearing a child. I put it in my mind that I would somehow make it to the next stop, aptly named Hospital de Orbigo, a full 15 kilometers away.

It was 7:30 p.m. and dark when I arrived. Astrid was standing in the doorway again, only this time in tears. She had worried about me all day hoping I would be able to walk. She prayed that afternoon for my safety and apologized for leaving me behind. She took my backpack and showed me the way to the small kitchen where there was at least a space heater for warmth. I dropped into the chair, completely exhausted from the ordeal. Astrid made me a tea and helped to take my boots off. Without mentioning it, we both knew that she had learned a great lesson to never walk past a pilgrim in need. With each lesson I had experienced throughout this journey, I had gained a respect for the mystical nature of the Camino.

a miracle on cebriero

O'Cebreiro was the place where Octavium Augustine entered the region of Galicia, bringing it into the fold of the expanding Roman Empire. The *Codex Calixtinus*, a 12th century pilgrim's guide refers to O'Cebreio as Mons February but in other texts it's shown as Zebruaril or Munt Febrayr. The word Cebreiro holds a long list of historical connections most often mysteriously related to the month of February. Ironically, the same month as the feast of St. Valentine; a celebration of love.

One of the first stories I read about the history of the Camino told of a miracle that happened on the mountain, Cebreiro, in the region of Galicia near the end of the Camino pilgrimage route. There was a priest who performed mass in a stone church, Santa Maria de Real, at the top of the mountain. In the summer he was busy with the constant arrival of pilgrims, but the winter months brought only a few local farmers. He felt insignificant and discouraged that his time was being wasted. One winter morning, the priest was going through the motions of saying mass to an empty church. As he raised the host up to the Lord, he felt a warm sensation filtering throughout his cold hands. Miraculously, the host turned into a piece of flesh. Then the wine in the chalice on the altar turned into blood. Seeing the body and blood of Christ, the priest devoted the rest of his life to serve the pilgrims and the people of the mountain. There is a statue of the Virgin Mary in the church and the Virgin's head is angled slightly, in acknowledgment of the miracle.

I don't believe in miracles, but the priest's story resonated with me and I was sure something special was waiting for me on the mountain. I could relate to his anger and emptiness because I had recently lost passion for the way I was living my life. I wasn´t experiencing my senses anymore, becoming numb with the fast pace of family life in the city. People always commented on how much passion I displayed in everything I did. I knew my true passion was a gift I was given to be used for a greater purpose. Until I could clearly define that purpose, I had been content to use passion in the areas of my life that were important to me at the time.

I believe passion is the driving force that aligns with one's purpose. Without purpose, there is no passion. Without passion, there is no purpose. I was determined to use my wisdom and special gifts to accomplish something more meaningful in the world. The mountain of Cebreiro held a special significance to me. I thought the priest's frustration could be related to his loss of passion, too. Had he resorted to blindly going about the rituals expected, based on his role as a clergy in the church? Could it be possible that he was afraid to face his deepest fear, too? This story profoundly connected with me and I was sure something was waiting for me on the mountain.

In the past if I dreamed about achieving something, it

often brought disappointment or sometimes failure because the outcome wasn't what I had expected. Now I was walking the Camino without expectations and more importantly, I had completely detached myself from the outcome. Thankfully, in my life no one expected me to become a pilgrim and when I did, no one knew what to expect from me at all. This freed me from my usual desire to please others.

As I walked that morning, I raised my head, and looked into the distance in worship. For most of this journey I had been looking at the ground ahead of me, in search of something. My state of willed surrender evolved and with my upraised eyes, I could now view the magnificence of the universe in front of me, from the perspective of a pilgrim walking four kilometers an hour.

The distant snow-capped mountains appeared to be only two or three centimeters high. Walking at this pace gave the appearance that the majestic mountains were growing in grandeur in front of my eyes. It felt as though I was walking into the mountain and drawn by the energy of its power together with its magnificent beauty. I was becoming one with the mountain. Nearing Cebreiro, I fantasized about the glory of reaching the mountain imagining all of the love of the universe flowing toward me. I thought if this love was within my being, surely from that place I could acknowledge my greater purpose in life.

Leaving the village of Marius de Rechivaldo that morning, the day was filled with sun and warmth. The terrain became more hilly and forested, a welcome change from the unvarying flatlands of the Meseta. Astrid, the Swiss pilgrim, was walking with me and we talked about our respective plans once we returned home. Astrid said that she thought it was important to live your dreams, but first one must know what their dreams are.

We crossed a Roman bridge, entering the city of Astorga. Astorga is a large city that was once the chocolate capital of Spain. Chocolate was a daily staple in my pilgrim diet, but this city seemed to have lost it's love of the bitter sweet aphrodisiac. It is also the capital for the wine region of La Rioja and they definitely hadn't lost their taste for great wine. Today was Tuesday, market day and I loved to wander through the varied stalls of a local market. Arriving in the city, we saw Roman ruins and a building, the Palacio Episcopal, designed by the famous architect Gaudi.

My injured knee had been aggravated by the stress of walking on the flatlands of the Meseta. I had assumed this part of the journey would be easier, but it was even more difficult to walk on the hard pavement of the city streets. Shortly afterwards, Astrid and I agreed to walk separately and at our own comfortable pace.

The next 50 kilometers would involve a difficult uphill climb for at least 30 kilometers to the highest point of the entire journey. The path would pass through one of the most beautiful sections of the Camino, Galicia. At the highest point a steel cross, Cruz de Ferro, had been built to help the pilgrims find their way through the dense fog as they crossed the mountain ranges. Below and on the cross, pilgrims left personal memorials such as written notes, clothing, memorabilia and obvious keepsakes. There was a huge pile of stones built from an ancient custom practised by pilgrims, who bring a stone from their home country. I hadn't known about this ritual so I selected a stone from the path and climbed to the top. Instead of putting my sorrow into the stone, I placed my thoughts of Canada and I set it down near the cross. Then I went down to the edge of the mountain, a drop of almost 5000 feet overlooking Galicia, took my boots off and sat there. With no one in sight I started to imagine what would happen if I slipped and fell down the mountain, curious about how long it would take before someone found me. Unperturbed, I ate an orange, a chocolate bar, had a drink of water and then I stood up to start walking again.

I loved walking every day. The ritual had exposed me to a familiarity of the inner rhythm of my divine soul connected as a part of the whole universe. After hours of solitary walking, I arrived at the old village of El Acebo. The homes along the path were an old style with balconies that hung over the street. A woman walking cattle and sheep, forced me to slow down as she maneuvered them through the narrow village streets. I followed them through the village looking for the refugio. I was pleasantly surprised to find out the local bar was the refugio. To my shock and great pleasure, it was actually warm inside! Putting my things on the bunk-bed upstairs, I returned to the bar with my diary and money to buy dinner. While I was eating, Stefan and Roulin, a Spanish pilgrim, walked in. That day I had completed 34 kilometers mostly alone, so their company was a welcomed change. They joined me for red wine, since they had already eaten. Sleeping that night was incredibly peaceful. Again, we were the only ones at the refugio.

The next morning by 7:30 a.m. I was on the road. Later I again met up with Stefan and Roulin at a bar and we had café con leche, but that was the last time I saw anyone for almost 40 kilometers. Many times along the way, I stopped in the bars to have a café or something to eat, hoping I would meet someone. Eventually my knee completely seized and I could no longer bend it. My journey was going very slowly.

Soon darkness fell and I struggled to find my way to the refugio in Villafranca de Bierzo. Entering the village, I came upon the Church of Santiago, where there was the famed "Puerta del Pardon." This is the door of forgiveness where pilgrims who were unable to walk any further, could be granted the indulgences of completing a pilgrimage. For a moment, I considered the prospect of going into the church for a pardon. Walking up to the door, I put my hand on the doorknob and turned it, but it was locked. I laughed to myself, assuming obviously this was an idea instigated by the devil. A big sign in front of me that I had not seen said the church was closed. Turning away, I walked back up the path and found a refugio directly across the road. A welcome sight.

When I opened the door to enter, I found a young man standing there and I said, "Hola" and he said "Hi." I was instantly relieved to hear English and noticing his accent, I asked, "Are you Canadian?" and he replied that he was. For a moment, I felt like I was home. I slipped off my backpack as we began exchanging a light-hearted conversation about Canada. His name was Kyle. He was young, had dark hair and was very good looking. He registered me, stamped my credential and then I gave him a donation. He offered to carry my backpack upstairs to the bunkroom and I gratefully accepted. When we reached the top of the stairs there were two doors. He asked, "Which room do you want to go in?"

I was puzzled by his question but so tired that I just said,

"It doesn't really matter, let's just go into the room that is closest." And that was the room on my right. I wouldn't appreciate the significance of this decision until later. Kyle opened the door and I went into a large room filled with about 30 bunk-beds. It was poorly lit and definitely cold. Nobody else was staying in the room. I picked out a top bunk along the wall on the left, unpacked my things, rolled open my sleeping bag and then went downstairs to have a shower.

Most of that day I had walked alone climbing into the mountains of Galicia, passing the highest point of 1517 meters, virtually 5000 feet. I struggled to walk down the steps, keeping my injured knee straight to avoid the agonizing pain each time it was bent. I knew from experience my muscles would recover by morning. An incredible lightness was experienced once unburdened from the weight of my boots and backpack. The stairs appeared to be built outside the building, which meant it was unlikely there would be any heat in the showers. I dreaded the thought of being wet and cold again.

As I suspected, the shower room wasn't heated and the evening temperature outside was hovering around freezing. I felt the cold air instantly and my entire body reacted, the muscles tensing at the thought of stepping barefoot onto the cold tile floor. I prayed there would be hot water. Quickly stripping off all my clothes, I left them on a hook outside the shower stall. Carefully stepping into the shower I pushed the button to release the hot water. Standing naked, I waited completely exposed on the cold tile for what seemed like minutes, before the warm water finally showered over me. I looked up in gratitude reminding myself, a pilgrim must always say thank you.

My mind softened as I stood there, the water flowing over me. I had almost no physical strength left. I gently caressed my fatigued body with the lather of the same green shampoo I used for washing my hair, body and clothes. I could feel the muscles in my thighs had become elongated but firm. My calves were solid as a rock with a new slimmed down shape, defined by the activity of walking. My feet tingled, freed from the restriction of my stiff leather hiking boots. Standing there my tired body wavered, too exhausted to maintain balance.

Mindlessly, I looked down and was mesmerized by the water rushing around my bare feet. It suddenly stopped flowing and was replaced by ice cold air. In a panic, I immediately hit the button to turn the hot water on again. Just as serenity returned along with the warm water, I pondered the simple pleasures of being a pilgrim. Without warning, the timer stopped the hot water from flowing. I grabbed my little high-tech chamois towel and dried myself. The towel only covered a small area at any given time, leaving me with a lot of unpro-tected wet skin exposed to the cold air. I found myself fantasizing about being wrapped up in a big fluffy white velour housecoat wearing warm furry slippers, sitting on a sofa with a heating pad and a glass of wine. Then harsh reality returned. Instead of a comfy robe, I covered my freshly scrubbed skin with my old, cold, dusty hiking clothes.

Climbing into the top bunk, I slipped into my sleeping bag to get warm and stop the shaking from a chill that had settled deep into my bones. After a few minutes, the shivering sub-sided as my body temperature began returning to normal. Sitting up, I looked around the room to find I was still alone and decided to go to town and buy food for dinner. Once downstairs, I could see that the main room had a huge fire-place, a bar, tables and benches and a dining room for meals. This was definitely one of my favorite refugios. I opened the door to go outside and there was a little white dog jumping about excitedly. I scratched behind his ears and said, "Hey buddy, how're you doing?" Assuming that the dog understood Spanish, I talked to him in a expressive voice so that he could understand. I straightened up and started to walk toward the village. He followed me everywhere, waiting outside each shop until I returned. It was like having my own little village host.

Having picked up supplies for the journey into the mountain, I felt at ease as I returned to the refugio. When I opened the door to go inside, sitting there at the table was the German pilgrim, Andreas. He was the pilgrim I met at the beginning of my journey who had told me the story of the sorrow stones; a tale that had a profound impact on my life. Seeing him I was overwhelmed by a feeling of ancient recognition, as though I had just met my oldest, dearest friend in the whole world. All I could say was, "Hi." My voice crackled and for the first time, I noticed the steel blue color of his eyes glaring naked behind the stylish glasses he wore. Time slowed down with a gradual calming effect. I asked if he had eaten dinner and he had. I recalled that there was an exceptional wine selection in this region so I invited him to join me at the bar, once I had finished my dinner. He accepted. I quickly ate in anticipation of a conversation with this intriguing pilgrim.

They sold bottles of great Spanish red wine at the refugio, so we decided to buy a bottle and stay there. Sitting alone at a table in the common room, near the warmth of the roaring fireplace, we drank the wine and shared our stories. The first thing I mentioned, was the impact his delightful story about the sorrow stones had on my journey. I told him about the ritual I followed everyday. It was my belief that the act of putting my sorrow and the sorrow of others into the stones, opened my heart for more love. I was surprised when he said, "You know I don't actually believe in sorrow stones." Stunned by this comment I couldn't speak. This ritual had changed my life. "It's just a story," he said, "a friend told it to me and I was sharing it with you." Hearing this, I came to a full realization of the true power of hope. It was my faith in the possibility I could put sorrow into a stone, and leave it on the Camino to create more love in my heart that made it real for me. It didn't matter if Andreas believed in the stones or not. It's just a story. In the end it's whatever I believe that really matters.

Andreas and I talked about our experiences. We described the people we had met along the way and what we learned from each of them. Time passed quickly. It was after 11:30 p.m. and the other pilgrims had gone to bed. We had a big day tomorrow as we both had plans to walk up the mountain of Cebreiro. We decided to call it a night and together we went up the stairs to the bunkrooms. At the top of the stairs we said goodnight. Andreas went into the room on the left and as I turned to go into the room on the right, for the first time I noticed a sign on the door that said, "This room for pilgrims over forty years of age!" Now I understand why Kyle asked me which room I wanted to sleep in because he was too polite to come out and ask if I was over 40 years of age. He was Canadian after all. By inadvertently choosing the room that Andreas was not allowed to enter, I was certain to be sleeping alone that night.

Removing my clothes in the cold air sent my body into shock and I broke out in goosebumps. Climbing up to the top bunk, I got into the cold sleeping bag, hoping it would heat up quickly. My mind floated into a deep healing sleep in anticipation of the next day. I was excited and nervous at the same time wondering what was in store for me.

The next morning, I joined Andreas, the Swiss and the Belgium pilgrims for a hearty breakfast prepared and served by the volunteers at Ave Fenix. This refugio is operated by D. Jesus Jato and his family who have devoted their lives to serving the needs of pilgrims. They also offered to take our backpacks by car to the top of the mountain, for a donation of course. Since my knee injury was still a concern, I wanted to have a break from carrying the extra 25 pounds uphill. Andreas eventually conceded.

Walking without our backpacks was strangely awkward at first; it was like leaving a part of our body behind. However, we quickly grew accustomed to the lighter load as we left the refugio ready for the most difficult part of the journey, a 1200 meter ascent walking a total of 28 kilometers. Somehow there was a feeling of security associated with carrying my backpack knowing that I had everything I needed to survive. It was like a part of me and now I felt bare, exposed to the elements. I was certain, this would be a test.

We looked at Andreas' detailed map to determine the best route. I was content to follow the yellow arrows that pointed the way to Santiago. Initially he seemed contrary, preferring to follow a map, so we agreed to meet for lunch and started out walking together with the understanding that we would eventually go our separate ways. Ten minutes turned into an hour; an hour turned into two and so on. Before we knew it we continued to walk together without question, telling stories and laughing. I truly enjoyed his company. In anticipation of something profound happening on Cebreiro, I didn't want to be alone on the mountain.

Andreas wore a dark blue coat and gray walking pants that hugged his perfectly shaped long muscular legs. His dark hair blew around lightly in the winter wind. Even as we walked side by side, I felt as though I could see the reaction on his face as I recounted stories of my experiences on the Camino and at home. He loved to hear stories and reveled in the art of storytelling as well, often sending us both into laughter with his animated tales. There was an innocence to his outward expression and genuine passion for life through the love of language, music, reading and theater. He touched the youth of my heart. Mesmerized by the sound of his voice and the graceful movement of his hands as he spoke, my imagination was free to create romantic ideals in my mind about the differences between North American and European men.

This day seemed no different than any other day. We took our time walking, often stopping to admire the mighty mountains. The countryside is beautiful in this region. With a rich green landscape wet with Galician rain, it's just like being in Ireland. Our walking pace had slowed down as night started to fall. We could see a village up ahead that must be Cebreiro and we were relieved that we didn't have far to go. It was almost completely dark when we arrived at a deserted village finding a sign that said, "Cebreiro 4 kilometers." "What are we going to do now?" I asked Andreas. Looking blankly at each other, we were seriously concerned about our safety walking up the mountainside in the dark. We didn't have a flashlight or any equipment with us since we had accepted the offer at the refugio in Villafranca for our backpacks to be driven to the top of the mountain. I had to talk Andreas into agreeing to do this and now I worried our lives were in danger. Four kilometers would take at least an hour of walking if we were on relatively flat land, but this was a steep mountain incline that never seemed to end. It was almost 6:00 p.m. so we wouldn't arrive at the refugio for a least a couple of hours. There was no other option but to continue walking in the dark. Fear for my life released a rush of adrenaline awakening all of my senses.

My eyes adjusted to the darkness as it descended upon us. Without the distraction of streetlights the natural glow of the moon lit our way. Like a gift from heaven, there were tiny white stones all a long the path up the mountain side. The moonlight touched the surface of these stones reflecting just enough light onto the path to be able to see the way.

Almost two hours later we finally arrived at the summit of the mountain. We entered the refugio to find two pilgrims; the Belgian woman, Delphine and the fast-walking Swiss pilgrim, Alois. We all shared stories of climbing the mountain that day while eating the basic pilgrim meal of bread, cheese, jamon and a chocolate bar for dessert. After dinner Andreas and I went to the bar for some locally made cider and Santiago torte, a speciality of this region. A crackling fire was burning in the corner of the empty room, while Andreas told me about his grandfather's method of making cider. As he talked my mind wandered freely. Although I had promised myself from the very beginning that I was not on this journey to get into a relationship with a man, I couldn't ignore the feelings I was experiencing. Stretching my legs out below the table, my feet purposely rested beside his. It felt a bit like Bernie when he rested by my feet, befriending me in the bar. The effects of the cider made me a little more amorous so I suggested to Andreas we return to the refugio.

The bunk-beds in the refugio were pushed together, like a double bed but once our sleeping bags were rolled out, it looked less like we were sleeping in the same bed. I brushed my teeth and used the washroom. Feeling nervous about his closeness, I quickly stripped off my long sleeved shirt, hiking pants and socks, and slid into the cold sleeping bag in my underwear, wondering if Andreas had seen me.

Tucked in my sleeping bag, I turned to look at him and burst into a loud belly laugh that I couldn't control. He was wearing a silly reading light that was fastened to an elastic strap wrapped around his head, making him look like a miner. Despite looking absolutely ridiculous, I was becoming very fond of him. With a frisky grin, I tucked my head inside the sleeping bag and fell into a deep sleep in the comfort of laying beside my ancient soul friend.

15   my love story

I f I consider Dante's notion that the secret rhythm of the universe is the rhythm of love, and that all virtues and vices come from a place of love, then I must be following the right path.

The morning is my favorite time of the day. My tired body had recovered with a night of rest. I opened my eyes and listened to the sound of Andreas' breathing as he lay sleeping. My body completely still, sensitive not to disturb his precious sleep. I fantasized about a romantic love affair with this man.

In a dreamy state, I turned onto my left side so I could at least see him. My breath quickened as I admired each and every fine line of his attractively featured face. His eyelashes seemed longer than I remembered. Minutes passed like hours and I couldn't wait any longer. I was impatient and lonely. Softly, in a raspy voice I whispered, "Are you awake?" There was no reply. Asking him again, "Are you awake?" This time a little louder. Without any movement, he slowly smiled and in a hushed, sleepy voice said, "Almost." The way he answered confirming what I suspected, he was also fantasizing about a romantic encounter with me. I wondered where we were going that day. Was it to a place we had already been?

Eventually we got up and set about completing our own daily rituals. After I dressed, I rubbed petroleum jelly on my feet, put on my sock liners and hiking socks which I had left to air at the foot of my bunk bed. We loaded our backpacks, filled our water bottles, checked the map to plan the day and dressed warmly to go outside.

As expected, the Cebreiro fog everyone had talked about, rolled in. We decided to wait to see if it would burn off before we would attempt to cross the mountains. After breakfast we sat at a table in the kitchen, writing in our diaries. We left as soon as the fog lifted. As we walked a light mist lingered around us, restricting our view of the world beyond the mountain. That morning, I woke up refreshed feeling like there was a new world of possibilities awaiting me.

Andreas and I walked in perfect step, with the weight of our hiking boots hitting the uneven ground in concert like the rhythmic cadence of a soldier's march. I had a long stride making it easy for me to keep up with his step. In the movement of our arms, the fabric of our coats brushed lightly against each other igniting a spark of energy with our touch. There was a familiarity to the rhythm of our movement.

Soon, the soothing sounds of the Galician countryside filled our private pilgrim world with Mother Nature's music; the water flowing in the rivers, birds singing, the wind gently gusting as it rustled the last leaves of fall under our feet. It was as though we were dancing in the ballroom of the universe, wondering if sometime, somewhere, we had danced together before.

Clambering up the mountain in silence, Andreas and I

followed the path worn down by the continual stream of pilgrims before us. It seemed like a lifetime ago when I first met him on the Camino. My memory took me back to that moment in time.

It was a few days into the start of my Camino. The day before I met him, my leather hiking boots had leaked because of the wet snow. Wet feet are a curse to any hiker since the risk for blisters to develop is magnified. Remembering the details of that distant evening. I recalled arriving at the refugio in a miserable mood, aggravated because I had injured my knee coming down the Pyrenees in the snow. Every muscle in my body ached. Irritable and tired, I had no intention of making new friends or starting any kind of a relationship with a man. Preferring instead, to be alone in my journey, even if I was cold and wet.

That night, once inside the refugio, I scanned the room looking for the personal space I would call home for the evening. There was a bunk-bed next to a curtain that divided the room. Privacy was a luxury on the Camino so I selected this bed as mine. My sleeping bag was set out as my claim to the top bunk. I took off my boots and then went to have a shower. I walked past a man working at a big white laundry sink, expertly caring for his walking boots. Thankfully, it was a large room, filled with shower stalls, complete with hot water.

On my way back to the bunk-bed with a freshly scrubbed body and attitude, I again noticed the swift, efficient movements of the man waterproofing his hiking boots. He was handsome and young and it seemed to me he should be looking for a bar or a night club to go dancing. I presumed that he was on the pilgrimage just to have fun so I wanted to avoid any conversation with him. But I was desperate to do something about waterproofing my boots in case of more wet snow. So without even introducing myself. I quickly asked if I could use his waterproofing kit. "Sure, use whatever you need," he said politely. With a word of thanks, I took the kit and walked away.

Laying out a newspaper, I brushed the dried mud off my boots and then covered each boot with the sticky gel. I repacked his kit neatly and handed it back to him, with a quick thanks. I felt badly about judging him the way I had and in an attempt to redeem my humble pilgrim stature, I apologized to him for being curt. Attempting a warm smile, I held out my hand out and introduced myself. He didn't smile back but he shook my hand and introduced himself as "Andreas, the German." His deep eyes briefly connected with mine. Later that night, as luck would have it, it was Andreas who told me the amazing story of the sorrow stones, changing my life forever. This introduction seemed to have taken place a lifetime ago and yet only three weeks had passed.

Waking on the mountain, Andreas talked and my mind wandered. I loved listening to his voice even though I had promised myself this journey would not include a romantic relationship. I missed the physical and emotional aspects of being with a man. I dreamed about being together with Andreas. Having reached this point of the journey, I completely surrendered to the Camino. Because of this, I wasn't afraid of love in whatever form it appeared, except of course, a physical relationship with a man. This was a journey to my soul; a love affair with myself. Romance would have to wait.

On the path with Andreas, I talked about how I had been going into the "gap" while I walked. The gap being a place where all creativity begins; the place where there is no time or space. I believed that I had the potential to create all that I truly desired through the discipline of meditation and repeating intentions. Andreas wanted to try to experience this. I suggested we stand and turn our bodies to face outward, toward the mighty Cebreiro mountains. For me, the mountains provided a direct connection with a universal energy channel. We looked to the mountains and meditated with deep breathing to completely still our minds. By centering with a conscious awareness of the ground below our feet, we released our body, mind and spirit to the universe, in surrender. With our minds completely at peace, and our bodies open and accepting to receive, the point of creativity could be accessed. Facing the mountains, we stood with our eyes closed. I could feel the radiant energy from him and the mountains coming together. Then it happened. Time stood still. It was a feeling of ultimate freedom. There was no movement, no activity, no thought, no noise, no space. Just peace.

The taste of the Galician rain lingered on my lips while I stood there in the gap. Time stood still. Time is only the perception associated with defined objects passing. There were no objects passing and therefore nothing to measure. The early morning air stood motionless that day and the clouds hung low surrounding us like a blanket, drawing our souls tightly together. In a state of heightened awareness, I stood there completely surrendered and receptive to the energy of the Camino.

Andreas and I openly embraced the possibility that our souls had met before at another time and place. We brought our inner world to the surface through the physicality of our bodies and it was a glorious moment. Our souls touched. It felt as though his energy, his breath, his very soul was within me and a part of me. Would this be a great love story about two pilgrim hearts, a German and a Canadian, meeting on a path others had traversed for over 1000 years, falling in love forever?

Through conversations, but without actually speaking the language of the people I met on the Camino, I discovered I had a special gift; an intuitive ability to communicate with other souls. As a student of the eternal soul, I had an unquenchable desire to understand universal love. Up until now I had been unable to connect the degree of untapped love I had with the physical world I lived in. Because of this I was constantly frustrated by the limitations of my expressions of love. It was as though universal love was familiar to me, but I couldn't quite reach it. I wanted to feel the glory of this love in every cell of my body.

Then something happened. A spark of love ignited a warm rosy sensation filling my entire body. Enrapturing my heart, it rushed to enter each threshold of my physical body in search of my soul. Even as I longed to accept universal love, I resisted, fearing it was too much for me to indulge. The intensity of the experience was creating panic and fear in me. To defend myself, I sent the love away from me in the direction of the only person who was there, Andreas. Once the love had gone from me, I was relieved, although saddened that fear would deny me something so incredibly wonderful. Why was I afraid of the love I had intended for myself everyday since the beginning of this journey? Why was I denying myself that which I truly desired?

Seconds later, with more clarity and intensity, another spark of love enraptured my entire body as something divine and powerful with a mystical energy. This time, I didn't want to fight anymore and instead I surrendered to myself by letting go of any attachment I had to the outcome. A light had entered my soul leaving me in a natural state of grace, now able to feel God, as my own self-love.

"What's wrong?" Andreas asked.

Speaking slowly as though I had been stunned by a vision I said, "I am not sure but it's so incredibly powerful." Feeling as though I was going to collapse, I tried to gather my composure. I felt like crying but I was confused, unsure of what emotion to express. Was this self-love or something even beyond that?

Andreas said nothing more. To give me some time alone, he turned toward the path to start walking again. I was reluctant to leave but I knew I must follow him. Unable to comprehend the implications of this profound event, I just accepted it. By putting one foot in front of the other, as I had done so many times before, the familiar rhythm of walking launched me back into the present moment.

That night I wrote about the experience in my diary without any idea this might be the miracle I had been hoping for. I lay in the bunk-bed next to Andreas. While he read a book, I wrote my love story. The next day we were resting on a rock near a swift moving river when Andreas asked me to explain what happened on the mountain yesterday. He knew something profound had occurred and he was curious about my experience.

In slow deliberate words I described to him what happened on Cebreiro. I told him that universal love actually presented itself to me twice. The first time, I was afraid to accept it, still not prepared to face my fear. In my past if I received love, then I gave it away. In my panic to control the situation yesterday, I rejected the love by giving it away to Andreas. But like a mirror, he reflected the love back to me a second time. Knowing that I might never have the potential for this experience in my life again, I finally welcomed love in a state of surrender. By accepting absolute love, the alchemy of transition had occurred. A miracle perhaps?

Curious, I asked Andreas, "When I gave you all the love of the universe, why did you return it? Why didn't you keep it for yourself? He looked deep into my eyes and slowly said, "Because, it wasn't mine to keep." I truly believe that if Andreas had kept my love that day, I wouldn't have experienced universal love; the essence of the soul exposed in a state of complete surrender. Telling him about the experience helped to make it more clear to me. All of my life I had believed that love was only about giving and receiving. What I learned on Cebreiro that day, was how to be love.

That day Andreas' words repeated in my mind increasing the degree of clarity about self-love. I had been denying myself love because I thought I might never receive what I truly deserved, but now because of the Camino it was different. It felt like I had found something I lost a long time ago; a sacred home for my pilgrim heart.

Finally my mind was at peace. By being love, I now have the love of God that calmly flows for eternity, rather than a love that is held in control locked in the fear of the past or future possibilities. With three daughters I've always tried to share my love equally among them, as though it was something I could measure. This quantity of love was determined by what I received from others, less the love I gave away. It was like a deposit and withdrawal system that could run out at any time, and often it did. I felt as though their confusion as adolescents and my life pressures, tarnished our ability to reveal the depths of our love to each other without fear.

With two of my daughters not living at home, I wasn't privy to their daily physical presence and expressions of love any longer. That night on the Camino, while I wrote in my diary, it occurred to me that the act of being love was a gentle way of filtering the love I have for my daughters, transcending space and time. This was the answer to my maternal desire to continue to nurture my children and possibly other souls in the universe. By being love, my children didn't have to fear my love would ever end. This approach gives a new meaning to the words, *I love you forever*. All along the Camino my purpose had been to rigorously complete the rituals I had set out for myself. I had deliberately denied myself any possibility of emotional entanglement but this day on Cebreiro, I surrendered to the way. I surrendered to the divine soul within me, to guide me – to self-love. By experiencing absolute love as a way of being love, I am nourished.

The events of that day indelibly marked the beginning of two love affairs; one with a romantic pilgrim and one with myself.

Like the priest's miracle, my purpose now has passion and my passion has purpose. If I consider the notion that the mirror of the universe reflecting my soul is the mirror of universal love, then I must be seeing myself in every person. To reflect, is about mirroring the inside towards the outside. Therefore if I have self-love and reflect it on the world, then I can love others by loving myself. A love affair with myself and the world as my lover.

cinco dias hasta santiago

Five days to Santiago.

*T*he austere silence was stirred by the sound of our deep breathing as Andreas and I climbed the Galician terrain.

There is a music to the Camino; a deliberate drum that beats out the rhythm of nature's song. The cadence of our movement creates a vibration joined in the silence of the clouds, the whisper of the wind, the song of the birds and the obvious thump of hiking boots touching down on the same soil that had been walked over by millions before. Often Andreas and I would stop walking to admire the magnificent beauty. Hours of constant rain acted like a mantra arousing my senses and elevating the level of conscious awareness I was experiencing. Soon my skin began to take on the aroma of nature, absorbing the fresh scent of the rain soaked forest. I was becoming the Camino.

Arriving at the edge of the forest, we could see a village ahead. In desperate need of a place to dry our clothes and get warm, we chose the first restaurant we came upon. Once inside, we were delighted to see a huge crackling fire, filling the room with the atmosphere and warmth of Spanish hospitality. We sat directly in front of the fireplace on oversized wooden chairs that were set around a low table. The furnishings were of a rustic style, made with rough-hewn wood. Being the only people in the restaurant we took our boots off, placing them with our backpacks and coats near the fire to dry.

We were served by the owner, a cheerful middle-aged man who appeared at our table promptly. His Celtic features were hidden behind a dark complexion. He greeted us, his steel blue eyes squinting with laughter. He nodded his head and smiled, as if he knew we were lovers. I listened to the melody of his beautiful language as Andreas conversed with him in Spanish. He spoke in Gallego, a local dialect. Andreas ordered "des bocadillos jamon y queso." The music of the language as they spoke sounded absolutely romantic. When I asked Andreas what he said that sounded so beautiful, he said dryly, "A ham and cheese sandwich." We laughed.

In Spain, most of these bars serve meals, café con leche, as well as a full bar with tapas all day. The Spanish still consider the afternoon siesta as sacred, creating problems for North American pilgrims who expect 24 hour customer service. It doesn't matter how hungry you are, they will not open a restaurant early. An alcoholic beverage, however, can be ordered any time, day or night, even during siesta.

The owner returned offering us a selection of complimentary tapas, a favorite Spanish appetizer made with cheese, olives, chorizo, sheep intestines and other delicacies. We drank the local cider joining in the relaxed manner of the atmosphere, commenting on the simple lifestyle of the people in this region. We ate our bocadillo and finished the meal with a café con leche. It was a wonderful way to spend a meal celebrating the beauty of life. We didn't want to leave but it was time to move on.

We had walked 27 kilometers in the rain that day. Departing the mountain ranges of Cebreiro we approached Samos; a medieval village known for a Benedictine monastery that boasts an ancient section that was built in the 6th century. Arriving in the dark, we managed to follow the yellow arrows to locate the door to the refugio. Entering we found an unheated, dark, gloomy room filled with bunk-beds. It was after 7:00 p.m. and a stern faced man appeared out of nowhere from the back of the refugio. Limping towards us, he announced vespers would be in ten minutes and that we should attend. Exhausted and chilled throughout, I just wanted to eat and go to bed. As tired as I was, I decided to be a part of vespers. With only enough time to brush my teeth and my hair, I joined Andreas. We stepped outside into the cold air that seemed to gnaw away at my normally good nature. We walked to the back of the building to be greeted by an elderly monk patiently waiting to escort us down the dark, hall into the chapel.

We decided to sit a couple of rows back, on the left. I stood close to Andreas, almost touching. He didn't move away. Instead he busied himself finding something to read. All of the monks entered together. Each had a personalized, ornately carved chair mounted on a raised platform, facing each other. Dressed in the traditional brown wool monk gown with a rope sash tied around their waist, it was apparent they had prepared for this moment with God. I, on the other hand, was just glad to be off my feet and sitting down. I put my boots on the kneeler, something when I was a child, we were never allowed to do in church.

The service began with a hymn. The monks rose to their feet and we followed. I was stirred by their angelic voices echoing throughout the little chapel. I looked up to see the same stern-faced monk, who told us to be at vespers, wagging his finger at me in disgust. Then he pointed to the prayer book, to suggest I should be reading the prayers out loud. Andreas handed me one but naturally it was written in Spanish. Raising my shoulders, I tried to communicate my lack of comprehension to the monk. It was no use. His eyebrows moved closer together and his face turned deep red in anger. He was not impressed with me and it was doubtful that I would be receiving any special blessings from the church on this day. The prayers ended rather quickly followed by a blessing for the pilgrims.

With their heads bowed, the monks left the chapel in an orderly procession, executed with precision. As pilgrims, we respectfully followed them out of the chapel into the dark hallway towards the refugio. Overhead lights hung from the high ceiling, illuminating our way as we joined the procession. There was just enough light to be able to see the gorgeous old paintings that covered entire sections of the stone walls as we passed.

Without warning, the seven monks parted, walking one by one to the opposite sides of the hallway. The last monk, the one who reprimanded me, took a position in the middle of the hall. As one, they began to move forward following an ancient ritual as if they had practiced it for a lifetime. With the gentle swing of their body, the weighted fabric of their robes swayed from side to side, fading in and out of the darkness in unison. I felt as if I was transported back in time. It appeared as if these same men had silently walked in the same order, taking the same steps, passing on the traditions of a faith, day after day, for over a thousand years. A continuum of faith and an offering of prayer to God and to pilgrims. Simultaneously, Andreas and I stopped walking and turned to each other as if to ask, "Did you just see that?"

Each time I arrived at a monastery, I noticed the monks seemed almost desperate for pilgrims to attend vespers. I wondered if they missed celebrating with the thousands of pilgrims seen in the summer months, since it was their calling to serve them. Watching them perform their rituals, I wondered if they were also waiting for a miracle to happen, like the priest on Cebreiro. The monks reminded me of the pilgrims I had met along the way. They had served us with their prayers. In return, we served them by attending the vespers. Astrid and I had learned on the Camino never to walk past a pilgrim in need. That night in our own ways, the pilgrims and the monks were taking care of each other's needs.

I slept alone in the lower bunk-bed against the damp cold stone wall. As the night went on the stone seemed to get colder, making the room very uncomfortable. Andreas was in the bed across from mine, only about five feet away. A mere three days had passed since we started to walk together, yet that night I felt that like I had known him forever. I got up early and went to use the bathroom. Delphine, a Belgian pilgrim we had met earlier that day, was already awake and busy preparing a breakfast feast of cheese, jamon, crackers, fruit, cereal and juice, laid out on a cloth placed over a small table.

I noticed Alois, her Swiss pilgrim companion wasn't in the bunk-bed, although his sleeping bag was. Delphine looked so sad. I asked her what was wrong. She told me that Alois had left unexpectedly in the middle of the night and hadn't returned. She tried to follow him but he demanded that she go back to the refugio, preferring to be alone. She worried for him all night as she knew of his private struggles with his own demons. Delphine was concerned about where he was and if he was cold. I offered to help but she assured me there was nothing I could do.

Andreas and I packed our things once again in preparation for the day ahead. Outside, it was sunny and clear, a perfect day for walking. Andreas took out his map to check the route. "I have a suggestion." I said, "Andreas, why don't we try something different. Let's just travel today without checking the map. The yellow arrows will show us the way and besides, then it will be more like an adventure, rather than charting a hike. Let's discover our way to Santiago, together, without any expectations."

"But I like to know what to expect," he said, "my guide is the best you can buy and the maps are quite detailed, making it almost impossible to get lost."

"That's my point. Put the map away and let's just see what happens. If we get lost, we can rely on the people and the given situation at the moment to guide us. Let's really go on a journey of discovery into the unknown." My voice was filled with idealized enthusiasm. "Trust me, we will find the way." I knew this because this was how I had travelled from the beginning. With some persuasion, he finally agreed to put his map book away and venture into the unknown with me.

Before we left Samos, we walked around admiring the architecture of the monastery. Locating a yellow arrow, we took the road out of the village. Within minutes of leaving, we noticed a man sitting cross-legged on a stone, under a shelter just off the path. We got closer and realized it was the Swiss pilgrim, Alois. He was meditating. I couldn't believe this was the same power walking Swiss pilgrim who sped past me in Hontanas. Maybe he was just now reaching his own Meseta, the place of transformation. We started to walk back to the refugio to tell Delphine he was there, but she was right behind us and could see him for herself.

As we walked away, we could hear Delphine desperately call out to him. I told Andreas, that my heart ached with her pain. He asked what I thought would happen to their love affair. With pensive consideration I said, "Delphine wishes to serve the Swiss pilgrim. She is a woman, with a maternal desire to nurture his soul with unconditional love." I said, intuitively understanding this woman's passion. "I think Alois is refusing to acknowledge her love, believing it will never end. He is over-confident and because of this, he centers his mind in a desperate search for his own inner peace, neglecting her needs. The more she loves him, the more he becomes exceedingly confident she will never, ever go away."

I ask Andreas to speculate what he thought would happen. He created his story. "She is really a dolphin." We laughed together at this playful pun on her name. "She is longing to return to her underwater home in the great blue sea. Right now she is a pilgrim walking westward under the stars of the Milky Way on a personal quest to reach Fisterre, the end of the world. On the way she finds a great lover, Alois.

She tells him that she is in love with him, but he tells her he is not on the Camino to have a love affair. Her passion in life is to find her true love. Right now, Delphine doesn't realize her true love can only be found, under the sea."

I carried on from there, "Delphine is a strong independent woman, she is respectful of his needs but she won't easily give up on this love because she believes in her heart, he is her true love. She only wants to serve him. She will wait until he refuses her love. Then she will return to the sea, never, ever to come back to him." We both sighed and laughed gently at the development of our serial love story.

We arrived in Ferriora. Again, that night we slept in bunk-beds beside each other. I told Andreas I had never slept next to a man for three nights in a row, without any physical contact.

"Are you complaining?" he said with nervous laughter.

"It was just an observation," I said.

The next morning I woke up first again. I whispered, "Are you awake?" There was no answer. Andreas stirred slightly and then I asked again, "Are you awake?" He said "Yes," and turned to look at me. With a warm smile on his face he said he loved the morning with me because I was always in a good mood. We lay there talking for about an hour. Finally, we had to get up to prepare for that day's walk.

Later that morning we arrived in Portomarin, a city that used to be located on the banks of the Rio Mino but which had to be moved when the river was dammed in the early 1960s. Prior to the flooding, the people wanted to save the Romanesque church, San Nicholas. They disassembled the church, and carried each piece up a steep set of stairs, stone by stone, to the top of a hill. The porto for this church was built by Master Mateo, who built the famous Portico de la Gloria in Santiago. The church, which now sits proudly in the town square, is surrounded by modern buildings. Although it paled in comparison to this miraculous feat of disassembling and rebuilding their historical stone church, I picked up a stone, put my sorrow into it, carried it up the stairs, and left it on the steps outside the church. Each day I continued to pick up stones and carry them for a while. I truly believed this ritual had changed my life. Each time I put sorrow in a stone, it gave me more new hope.

Outside of the city, we trudged along the ancient muddy path lined with dark moss-covered stone walls, leading us into an enchanted Galician eucalyptus forest. It was a glorious sunny day so I suggested we get some food and cider. We were heading into a forest that would be a perfect place to have a picnic. We bought standard pilgrim fare; fresh bread, jamon, cheese, olives, pears, chocolate and cider. The forest was filled with giant oak trees, the kind found illustrated in Druid tales and fairy books. We walked deep into the woods and entered a romantic fantasy world only weathered pilgrims could truly appreciate.

The sun was blazing through an opening in the forest canopy onto the floor below. We both stopped walking at the same time; this was the place where we would feast. Laying our jackets out as a makeshift picnic blanket, we unpacked the food placing it on the bags it came in. We broke the bread with our hands and used our knives to cut the meat and cheese. The black olives added a strong Galician flavor, to the feast. Andreas opened a bottle of cider for each of us and we toasted our Camino life. It was perfect.

When we finished eating, I lay down resting my head on

my backpack and I looked beyond the tree tops to the blue sky, watching the leaves gently fall to the ground. At no other time in my life have I felt so completely a part of the universe; something bigger than the world I entered when I was born. The Camino was like shaking hands with the universe, as it welcomed me into a world far beyond the limitations of the ego. Suddenly, a bird chirped. Andreas heard it too and he smiled at me saying, "The Camino is acknowledging you." I started to daydream that instead of laying on my backpack, my head was laying on his chest. I could feel the beating of his heart. By intending and imagining the feeling of loving myself, I had found self-love. Now it seemed like I could imagine the feeling of Andreas' love, and find love there too.

It was now Tuesday December 4, 2001. Only two days were left before we would reach our destination, Santiago. We had slowed our pace considerably. At times we walked in silence, at other times we talked incessantly. Whatever we did, it was always perfect, for that moment.

It is dark again when we arrive in the city of Melide, famous for its seafood, especially *pulpo*; a local dish made of fresh, spiced octopus. We followed the yellow arrows to the refugio, registered and showered. In my *Confraternity of St. James Guide*, they recommend finding a bar that offers all-you-can-eat pulpo. It is served on wooden platters with a carafe of white Ribeiro wine. We found a place on the main street called Casa Pulperia Exequiel that looked interesting. There were pictures on the wall of the restaurant in the summer, bustling with hundreds of customers being served. We seemed out of place as the only patrons in the huge restaurant filled with long wooden tables and benches but they didn't seem to mind. The owner spoke some English and had been to Canada, sharing everything he knew with us. The woman who was cooking, told us she had been making pulpo at this pulperia for 35 years. We knew the food would be exceptional and it was. That night we drank wine and ate far too much pulpo. Struggling to move, we finally rose and walked back to the refugio. Back to the simple life of being a pilgrim.

I knew I wouldn't deviate from my intention to not have a romantic love affair on the Camino. I was so close to the end of my journey I couldn't give in now, although I was giving it serious thought until Andreas started to snore and very quickly, I fell asleep.

17

mount joy

ne more day before Santiago. My guidebook mentioned an outlying village where pilgrims of the past traditionally bathed before entering the city of Santiago but we had missed seeing it despite having walked slowly all day. We had visited all of the cafés and bars along the way, however, trying to prolong the remaining hours of our journey.

It was night and we were walking on the dark shoulder of the highway looking for a refugio. We couldn't be seen, putting our lives in near constant danger. Cars and trucks whipped by us at 120 kilometers per hour. The slipstream from the oncoming traffic was so strong that it shifted the weight of our backpacks as it passed, twisting our bodies out of control. In the dark there was no way to see the yellow arrows and even Andreas' map wasn't accurate. I prayed to the Camino to keep us safe. Trusting Andreas, I walked directly behind him, mirroring each step he took. Finally stopping at a small store Andreas asked for directions. We were assured the refugio was only 500 meters up the highway so we continued. A half hour later, there was still no sign of any refugio.

A newer building set just off the highway came into sight. It was the refugio. Checking the door, we found it locked. A note was posted showing a phone number to call and thankfully, there was a pay phone nearby. Andreas called and a woman answered saying she would be there in ten minutes. We sat outside in the darkness, just happy to be safe from the speeding traffic. A small-framed shy looking woman arrived to unlock the door. She accepted a donation, stamped our credentials and politely left. I was overjoyed to find there was heat in the bedroom. To my further delight, there was a free-standing white bathtub in the middle of the huge bathroom. This was a special moment; I have been waiting 27 days for a bath. Generously, Andreas suggested I go first and of course, I accepted.

The sound of the running water had a comforting effect. Leaving my clothes in a pile on the floor, I gingerly slipped into the hot bath. I laid back, resting my head against the cool enamel letting out a glorious sigh of relief. The hot water warmed my tired muscles, aiding in their recovery. Laying there, I was a contented Pisces lady in the midst of all her glory, my body and mind finally comfortable in a refugio.

My feet became *pruney* and the water started to cool down. It was time to let Andreas have a bath. I emptied the water, replaced the plug, and began to fill the tub for him. To my shock and horror, there was no hot water left! I gave him the bad news and then offered to give him a foot massage in exchange, which he gladly accepted. With absolute care, I held his foot gently, then firmly pressing my fingers into the pressure points on the soles of his feet, I massaged more deeply. There was no conversation, just complete relaxation on his part. This was the first time I had touched any part of his body and my heart raced. That night, despite the fact that we were the only souls in the entire refugio, I adhered to my intention and slept alone. I don't know how I did it.

The next morning we shared our food, eating yogurt and fruit for breakfast. It was Thursday December 6, 2001 and we were setting out to walk the last leg of our journey. The refugio in Santiago holds over 600 pilgrims and I was truly grateful that I would be sleeping only one more night in a cold bunk-bed.

It was sunny that day and we walked together without effort. The path was worn and there were markers along the way to let us know how many more kilometers remained to Santiago. As we got closer to the city our pace continued to slow down as a way of avoiding the inevitable.

Arriving in Monte de Gozo (also known as Mount Joy), I was disappointed with what had become a modern over-developed site for tourists. I read in my guidebook that Monte de Gozo is the first place on the Camino where the Cathedral in Santiago can be seen by the pilgrims approaching from the direction of the Camino Frances route. That must have been written a long time ago because now the view is overgrown with trees. Andreas and I stood there looking at the city streets below. I had been through a life-altering ordeal which filled my world with absolute love, yet somehow at this place, I felt almost no emotion. Definitely, I felt no joy.

With only seven kilometers left to walk, we moved past San Lazaro, where a leper hospital had been replaced by a chapel. Finally arriving in the city of Santiago, we walked through the typical residential and business areas of the city, on sidewalks and pavement that felt odd after walking the pilgrim's path through rural Spain for so many days. Still following yellow arrows and scallop shell symbols, we reached Rua San Pedro, in the old quarter of the city. Andreas turned to me and said, "I don't want to arrive in Santiago. I don't want the journey to end."

Then I replied in a naïve sort of way, "It's not the end of the journey, Andreas." I added with confidence, "When the Camino ends, the journey begins." The words continued to distill in my mind while walking in the direction of the Cathedral.

Approaching the absolute beauty of the building, we paused to allow our senses to take in the glory of the experience. I stared, virtually in a trance unable to take my eyes off the magnificence before me. This was a glorious moment. The journey, walking the path like millions of pilgrims before us, has ended and we have arrived at our destination. By covering 780 kilometers by foot and an untold distance in spirit, we have proudly earned the plenary indulgences and the honor of being pilgrims for the rest of our lives.

We paced around the Cathedral to find the special door where the pilgrims are to enter. Outside the door, we slid our backpacks off and sat down on a bench. The warmth of the sun beat down on us. Very few people were around. Anxious to relieve the overpowering emotion that had filled me, leaving my body weak, I took a deep breath and exhaled slowly. Andreas and I looked into each other's eyes in acknowledgment of our new found joy.

Sitting on the bench we were inspired facing that moment of truth. My body was still, gathering the intensity of the moment. Impassioned with emotion, I was overwhelmed with a sense of joy and Andreas and I embraced. Holding Andreas next to me, I was relieved and comforted by the beating of his heart so close to me. Listening with a heightened sense of awareness, I recognized the familiarity of his ancient pilgrim soul, wondering again if we had been together at some previous time.

I looked for a reaction from other pilgrims who had just completed their journey, but we seemed to be the only ones who had just arrived. We stood slowly while trying to gather our thoughts and emotions. Swinging our treasured backpacks over our shoulders we began walking to the main square, the Plaza del Obradoiro. There, we were graced with the incredible sight of a golden facade adorning the impressive architecture of the Cathedral. The beauty before us led our eyes around, moving slowly to absorb the artistry of the glorious holy images. Climbing the stairs, Andreas walked over to the wall to leave his treasured walking stick hoping that another pilgrim would find the needed strength in it to embark on a new life journey.

We stepped inside the door and our eyes devoured the divine sight of the famous 12th century Portico de la Gloria; a pillared entrance designed by Master Mateo. I read that the Cathedral of Santiago de Compostela, was originally built as an open structure but because the pilgrims visiting began to sleep near the statue of the Apostle, it was eventually closed in. The Portico de la Gloria has been protected from the outside elements and therefore, it is immaculately preserved.

As you enter the Portico de Gloria, it is customary to place your hand on the Tree of Jesse under the statue of St. James, in thanks. This is where the hands of millions before us have worn the carved stone smooth, taking on the shape of a large hand print. As I placed my right hand on the cool stone,

I felt a sense of belonging with the many pilgrims who have been here before me. I was eternally grateful to the Camino and the Virgin Mary for bringing me safely home to Santiago. On the other side of the pillar there is a statue of Master Mateo, the architect himself. It is customary to bump heads with him while asking a question about life. In a mocking tone, I asked, "What next big guy?" Like the chickens in Santo Domingo, he didn't answer me, so I left.

Walking up the center aisle I felt the presence of God all around me. The magnificence of the architecture and historical significance of every work of art, left me feeling devout and in awe of the graceful beauty I beheld. Andreas and I joined an unusually short line-up waiting to climb the stairs to the top of the altar. We were to experience another historic ritual affectionately known as "A Hug for the Apostle." Here I could give thanks to all the people who had helped me along my journey, by dedicating this hug to them. Approaching the statue from behind, I wrapped my arms around St. James and hugged him in gratitude for all his blessings. Descending the stairs and still basking in the glory of the experience, we stopped to pay our respects at the tomb of St. James the Apostle.

After what seemed like hours of looking up into the nave of the Cathedral, we sought out the Pilgrims Office to obtain the Compostela certificate. Following Andreas' map, we walked through the old streets of Santiago, to the Rua do Vilar. Arriving at the building, we climbed the old wooden stairs and entered a large room through glass doors. I could just imagine the room filled with summer pilgrims. Today it was empty except for a young woman at the desk who would verify that we had completed the pilgrimage. I handed her my credential with the 29 stamps showing the stops along my journey. She told me that on the certificate, my first name would be translated into Latin. She wrote the name *Suzannah Kenney* stamped and signed the certificate. Then she told me that this name was an honor since it was St. Susanna and St. John the Apostle who were the co-patron saints of the city of Santiago de Compostela. Was I a saint after all?

Andreas received his Compostela next. Excited, I asked him what his name was in Latin and he said (with just a hint of sarcasm), "Andreas." He shrugged his shoulders and then told me it was shown in Latin as *Andream*. We both left proudly holding our certificates; proof we were officially pilgrims of the Camino. Like the gold medal won at the world masters regatta, I knew the certificate meant very little compared to the journey it represented.

At noon we attended the Pilgrim's Mass at the cathedral, sitting in the section allotted to pilgrims. I was anxious to participate in another ancient ritual. The Mass started and I reveled in the now-familiar music of the Spanish language. Admiring the detail in the statues of the saints, I gazed into their eyes. Driven by ecstatic passion it was apparent they could see their vision with clarity. They faced their truth with the courage and humility of a pilgrim. They faced their fear. After all, they were saints.

In this moment I reflected again on my Camino. I acknowledged that I had accomplished what I had set out to do. I had faced my deepest fear. By unselfishly loving myself and others, without condition, I ultimately embodied absolute love. By being love, I discovered self-love. Through self-love, I learned compassion. Through compassion, I became more enlightened. Through enlightenment, I learned the Camino is God. Through God, I am guided to my higher purpose.

Through my higher purpose, I inspire by sharing my light. By sharing my light, I instill absolute love. Through absolute love, I find peace. Through peace, I find joy.

Through joy, there is happiness. All I really wanted from the beginning of this journey, was universal happiness. On the Camino, I had finally found my way.

"Canada." A voice called.

From the pew I could hear the priest's voice clearly. It is customary to announce the mass for the pilgrims who have arrived in Santiago by naming their country. I knew the blessing was for me since I was the only Canadian among the eleven pilgrims who had arrived that day. The priest's blessing for this humble peregrina now confirmed this part of my journey was over. Emotionally moved, my eyes overflowed with tears of joy.

Andreas and I left the Cathedral for the Plaza del Obradoiro. We stood there admiring the Hostal de los Reyes Catolicos, a Parador hotel. Andreas was familiar with the luxury hotel chain throughout the country saying this was undoubtedly the most famous one in Spain. We looked at each other and immediately knew we had the same idea.

The outside of the five star hotel was ornate and opulent. It seemed strange to be dressed as a pilgrim going into such a sophisticated hotel. I felt so far removed from the world I had left, just one month ago, that the behavior and dress of everyday people fascinated me. Andreas settled the details for the hotel room and returned with a porter who carried our backpacks. It was an odd feeling to have someone else carry my load, but I was glad to be relieved of the duty and didn't complain.

Andreas opened the door to display a large bright room filled with exquisite antique furniture. Heavy brocade drapes framed the high windows beside a huge king-size bed. I was immediately happy to feel the room temperature was comfortably warm. Once the porter left, I ran to the bed and jumped up landing on my back, delighted it wasn't a bunk-bed. Andreas called for me to come quickly to the bathroom. He stood there with a big grin on his face admiring a crisp white bath tub, sitting there like a throne in all its glory. There were fancy sample bottles of shampoo and lotion that smelled like another world, so distant from the simple life of a pilgrim. It was comforting to know that this time when we took a bath, we would not run out of hot water.

From the first time we met, Andreas and I had both agreed to live our Camino life based on a philosophy to expect nothing, therefore everything is a gift. Over 29 days of walking I had resisted all temptations, emerging in a state of natural chastity. Our decision to stay at the Parador had confirmed our re-entry into the profane world off the Camino. By doing this we agreed to freely accept intimacy combined with our desire for romantic love. This evening would be a mystical marriage as we both surrendered to the passion of romance and our souls' longing to be one again. Our spirit acted in freedom as a communion of true love.

That night was a gift.

18

the road back home

I t is customary for pilgrims to meet at the Gato Negro Bar in Santiago. The narrow cobblestone road through the old part of the city leads us to the little bar huddled amid the tourist shops. Andreas and I stepped inside to the excited noise of voices filling the room. We made our way to the back, joining a party of pilgrims Andreas had met along the way. We were celebrating our new found life. It was just like being at a family reunion, except everybody liked each other!

We all feasted on deliciously prepared home-made Spanish seafood dishes and drank full-bodied red Spanish wine. A spirited energy filled the air as pilgrims enthusiastically exchanged their stories. Some spoke of their plans for the return back home, others of the soulful journey they had undertaken.

Ages ago it seemed, Dino had predicted that on the Camino we would recreate our bodies and recreate our minds. Now at the finish, everyone commented about how their own physical body had changed; weight they had lost or new muscles that had developed where none existed before. This was a change that everyone could plainly see. The journey to the spirit, however, couldn't be seen so easily. We would have to go home and experience what had been recreated in the mind, since it wasn't outwardly obvious.

Just then Stefan arrived and I jumped up to hug him. His face was filled with a radiant light reflecting the hope of every pilgrim, that surely inner peace will prevail.

Stefan had changed, becoming more mature than I remembered. There was a lively energy about him, that was unseen before. It was as though he had somehow transformed. It seemed every pilgrim at the restaurant that day possessed a special warmth, a light that shone from within.

Andreas and I shared a toast with all the pilgrims and then we left. We stopped at a café down the road that served *chocolate con churros*, a Spanish desert of long slim donuts dipped in a chocolate sauce. After dessert, we window-shopped leaving us in awe of the commerce of the modern day world we had left, so long ago.

Everyone has a love affair on the Camino. Andreas and I had fallen in love. Holding hands we leisurely strolled through the city as free spirits, living completely in the moment. Our time together was precious, cherished with the knowledge that tomorrow he would return to Germany, and I to Canada.

The next day we stopped at the Cathedral to attend Mass again. Afterward, we were blessed with the opportunity to see the swinging of the *botafumeiro*, a huge censer filled with pungent incense. It required the combined strength of six men pulling at large cables to produce enough momentum to swing the huge censer across the transept of the church. Emitting a strong scent, it was meant to cover the stench of the thousands of travel-worn and unwashed pilgrims. Luckily, there were only a few pilgrims present on this cool winter day and most had likely taken a shower recently.

We had one more final café con leche at an outdoor café where we unexpectedly met the power-walking Swiss pilgrim, Alois. He sat alone with a long-stemmed red rose laying in front of him on the table. Delighted at seeing a fellow pilgrim, we greeted him excitedly. Then he told us the news about Delphine. Apparently, he just found out she had decided to go to a convent to spend six months in meditative seclusion. He appeared to be very sad. Empathizing, we wished him a "Buen Camino" and left him sitting alone.

"The dolphin went back to the sea, didn't she?" Andreas asked with excitement in his voice.

"Yes, she has gone to find her true love," I said in an understanding tone. "I wonder about the rose. Do you think it was for her?"

"Of course! He finally realized his love for her, but maybe you were right, it was too late." We walked in silence. I thought about how fortunate we were to have found true love in each other. But, I wondered if someday, like Delphine, I would return to the sea alone.

We took a taxi to the airport and Andreas checked in. Finding a restaurant, we sat close together, savoring every second of the twenty minutes remaining before Andreas had to leave. We held hands across the table. Few words were shared, the intensity of our love alone filled the silence.

His flight was called. Our eyes met knowing that time had run out, mine filled with tears. At the security check lineup, we kissed passionately, like two lovers being separated forever, without regard for the people around. He pulled himself away from me. I turned to walk away as tears streamed down my face.

"Sue, I need you," I heard him call. I turned to see him calling me to come back. With all the changes for tighter security restrictions arising from the September 11 bombings in the USA, three months earlier, his utility knife had been confiscated. Andreas wanted me to have it.

I ran back, but by the time I got there Andreas was gone. I took the knife from the security guard and immediately left the airport.

Getting into a rented car, I checked the map to exit the airport parking lot. To complete my journey I would drive to Fisterra and then on to San Sebastian where I would board a train to Paris. It was lonely without Andreas. Standing by the lighthouse at the *end of the world* I thought about the prospects of integrating my new Camino life into the world back home. That night I wasn't allowed to stay at the pilgrim's refugio since I was no longer a walking pilgrim. There was a hostel nearby with lots of rooms available, where I spent the night alone.

The next day I drove along the northern coast in silence, making my way to San Sebastian. It is a gorgeous seaside city wrapped around the Bay of Biscay. I spent that day walking aimlessly around the old village often looking out to sea, wondering what Delphine had found and at the same time I was lonely for Andreas. It was an eight-hour journey on the train from San Sebastian to Paris, covering almost the same distance it had taken me twenty-nine days to walk. How my life had changed since that day I first met Jacques at the Pilgrim Office in St. Jean Pied de Port. I boarded the plane from Paris. Once in the air, I began to read my diary noticing the many gifts and lessons from the pilgrims I met and my own experiences on the Camino. I wrote each of the lessons on the last page of my diary listing a total of 55 gifts and lessons I had discovered over 780 kilometers of walking.

Walking is a state of being. On the Camino I was presented with the idea that the true pilgrimage is not just the physical aspect of the activity of walking, but the ongoing spiritual journey as well. I could not complete this or any other journey in my life, unless I was prepared to continuously put one foot in front of the other, even when it seemed I wasn't going anywhere.

Dino had said that a saint is someone who faces their fear. On the Camino, I faced my fear again and again. Cebreiro is a place where divine mystical love flows in the peacefulness of nature's beauty. There, I embodied absolute universal love with the strength of my passion ultimately driving me to face my deepest fear. I walked a million steps and I was now a pilgrim ready to embark on a new journey living my higher purpose. On the Camino I had found my sanctuary, that precious place in my soul where I could be love and fulfill my maternal desire to nurture others.

This is a place I dream of returning to again and again.

epilogue

Six months after I came home, my passion for the Camino was still evident in every part of my life. Andreas and I did our utmost to maintain our romantic love affair, despite the distance. I found myself telling my stories to anyone who would listen; friends, family, business groups, churches and complete strangers, too. My daughters joked that I had gone *luna Espana*.

To my surprise, my stories became popular. The tales that presented the idea of a pilgrimage as a metaphor for a life-journey with purpose, seemed to resonate with many of the listeners. The people expressed a desire to begin a simple approach to living a life more consistent with their values. To address this, I developed workshops to teach skills and practical applications of the pilgrim's way to going on a life-journey.

As part of my desire to share my pilgrim light, I also recorded a storytelling CD called *Stone by Stone*, about my experiences and the people I encountered on the Camino Frances. People wanted to know when I would be writing a book. Since I had kept a detailed diary of my walk and had been telling, re-telling and refining the stories for over a year, I decided it was time to start writing.

Back in the real world, I found the pace of city life was far too fast for me to concentrate. I gave away many of my personal belongings and furnishings, moved out and left Toronto. No longer burdened with an abundance of material things, I started a new pilgrim life taking up residence in a lakeside cottage near the Mnjikaning Reserve.

I was back in the rustic comfort of nature and I began to write. Two years have passed. I worked through the last winter and spring months in solitude, completing the manuscript for this book. Through writing it, I was reminded what I accomplished the first time I walked both spiritually and physically. People have been kind and generous in their compliments regarding my feat but to tell the truth, I felt a bit like Bernie, the legendary dog of the Camino. After he trotted 24 kilometers to the next village he didn't turn around and walk back. No, instead Bernie waited for someone to give him a ride back home. And me? It took a car, a train, a plane and an overpriced cab to get my sore feet back home. I decided if I returned to the Camino the next time I would walk in both directions, the same way my ancestors completed their pilgrimage to Santiago and back home again.

In March 2004, I got the urge to walk again. I checked my schedule and the flight availability to find out it was possible for me to go in early April. I bought a return ticket to Vigo, Spain with plans to do the Portuguese Route and walk in both directions. Two days after booking the flights, I sent an email announcing the details to my friends.

The Camino is calling again.

I will finish the manuscript edits for my book by April 3, 2004. On 04/04/04, I will leave to fly to Vigo, Spain. From there I will travel to Ponte de Lima, Portugal to begin my walk on the Portuguese route of the Camino. I will arrive in Santiago on Easter Sunday and since 2004 is a holy year, the celebrations of the Passion will be incredible.

The next day I will begin an 87 kms walk to Fisterre, on the west coast of Spain; a place the medieval pilgrims believed was the end of the world. Then, I will walk back in the direction I just came from; first to Santiago and then on to Portugal. The entire round trip covering roughly 500 kms.

Please send me your intentions. Intentions are your wishes, dreams, prayers, thoughts or anything you want for yourself, someone else or for the universe. I will put all the intentions I receive into a stone and take it with me to leave in Santiago.

May you find peace and love on your journey.

Sue

That same day, I received an urgent reply from a dear friend.

Sue,

I had a dream about you. In the dream I was given a message to deliver to you, before you leave on your journey. I must see you.

Sherry

Sherry had befriended me shortly after I moved from Toronto, garnering my utmost love and respect. The first time I met her we were both keynote speakers at a business conference. Following my speech, she immediately came to me and put her hand out to shake mine. Sporting a big smile, she said, "Hi Sue, my name is Sherry. I'm truly impressed by your story and your big city style," she teased, handing me her business card. "Please call me, I would like to buy you lunch." That was the introduction to a dear friendship that has since developed between us.

Sherry is from the Chippewas of Mnjikaning the First Nation, the daughter of a Chief. Highly respected as a mother, business woman, storyteller and active champion for Native rights, she is truly treasured in the community.

We arranged to meet a few days later. When Sherry arrived we talked about our personal life philosophy and values. She said she had something for me to take on my journey. Then she presented me with a package that was flat, covered with red fabric and tied with a piece of deer skin. As I opened it, she told me that her people were from the Deer tribe. I unfolded the red fabric and opened a cardboard sleeve to find an perfectly elegant feather laying there. I picked it up and held it in front of my heart embracing it. I knew what it was and I was deeply honored.

"It's an *eagle feather*," I said, my entire body filling with its powerful energy.

Sherry nodded and smiled with great pride. "I was told to give it to you." she said.

"Can you tell me what happened in the dream?" I asked anxiously.

"You were on your journey. You were all dusty. You were speaking to someone about a matter of great importance. In the dream, there was a vision of a message I am supposed to give you." She paused, confirming my absolute attention. She spoke clearly and deliberately.

"You are to take this eagle feather with you on your journey. While you are holding the feather, you are in direct contact with the Creator. You must be sure it doesn't come into contact with anything that changes the natural state of the mind. Do you understand?"

I nodded and listened intently as she gave me more instructions.

"You will give it to a person, who is not from where you are from. This person will take the eagle feather to a place, that is not from where they are from." She paused.

"How will I know who is the right person?" I asked, suddenly concerned with the burden of being responsible to choose the right person for this highly distinguished honor.

"You will know, Sue. Just remain open and willing to receive. The person will present themself to you." I nodded waiting for more instructions. She went on to say, "Do not concern yourself with probing questions to make sure a person meets the right criteria. Trust that you will make the right decision as I trust you."

Overwhelmed with emotion, I stood there holding the

eagle feather, unable to move or speak. Sherry said, "You are safe and protected as long as you have the eagle feather in your possession." For a moment, I considered asking her if I could keep it for protection at least until I finished my journey but I didn't.

Imparting the tradition of her people, she spoke with clarity. "The red fabric will protect the eagle feather, as it is the universal color of the blood that flows in our veins. Red is also the color of the sunrise. This fabric will be its home. Each day you should hold the eagle feather to recharge its sacred energy. Know that the eagle flies the highest and sees the furthest of all creatures. An eagle feather acknowledges someone with gratitude, love and ultimate respect."

Then, beaming with pride she said, "My Nookomis (Grandmother) taught me that it is best to pray to the Creator just as the sun is rising. Always begin the prayer by saying, 'Miigwech Creator,' which means thank you Creator."

She looked at me with her deep brown eyes, speaking with assured grace, emphasizing the significance of these instructions. "Sue, you are being sent on this journey as a messenger, delivering an important story of our people. I know you will make the right choice."

We hugged, holding each other for a long time. I thanked her many times over. And then, quietly she gathered her things and left, leaving me with a precious eagle feather and a mission to find it a new home.

And so a journey begins ...

ABOUT THE AUTHOR

Sue Kenney's philosophy about life is that every thought, action and intention should come from a place of love. Fearlessly, Sue journeyed through intense weather conditions, walking alone in the winter months on a life-altering odyssey, with the intention of discovering self-love – something she had seemingly lost in a society that honors material goals and values.

Just five short weeks before she took her first step on the Camino, Sue's career was deemed redundant as an account executive with an international telecommunications corporation. Having spent 24 years in the telecom industry, she left the familiarity of her world to become a simple pilgrim like so many millions before her.

At the age of 40, a single mother with three children, Sue decided to learn the sport of rowing. Only six years later she was part of a crew of eight woman who won a gold medal at the FISA World Masters Rowing Championships. As a competitor she has been on the podium at a variety of regattas including Canadian Henley and the Canadian Indoor Rowing Championships.

Sue Kenney was born and educated in Toronto and now lives north of the city. She is a writer, international keynote speaker, training consultant and entrepreneur and lives the Camino in every aspect of her daily life, and through her work – she is truly, an inspiration to everyone who meets her.

Keynotes, Seminars and Workshops

Sue Kenney is a sought after international keynote speaker and training consultant, coach and entrepreneur. She has addressed thousands of individuals drawing on her wisdom from life-altering experiences acquired as a competitive Master's rower, a simple pilgrim and from a long career in the corporate world.

Sue offers a solid philosophical approach to providing personal and business leadership skills. She inspires others with powerful messages delivered through the art of story-telling. The design of unique life-skills workshops helps to further develop personal presence and authentic power, both to the private and public sector. Her stories have been featured on radio and television, and published in newspapers and magazines.

To book Sue Kenney for your next event or in-house workshop/coaching, visit www.suekenney.ca.

MESSAGE FROM THE PUBLISHER

I first met Sue Kenney in the late hours of the fall celebration by book and magazine publishers, writers, entertainers, associations, etc., who had been joined by White Knight Publications to display their latest publishing efforts at *Word On The Street.*

Well-stuffed booths filled Toronto's Queen Street from Spadina Avenue to University Avenue during the daylight hours allowing the crush of almost 200,000 visitors and book lovers to jam the roadway usually reserved for streetcars and automotive traffic.

Other than being attracted to her appearance and gracious smile, I was immediately drawn into a conversation about Sue Kenney's recent journey across the north of Spain, walking alone on a journey of great merit.

The life she had chosen to live as a spiritual mentor since leaving the world of commerce, her life as a world-champion rower, the Camino walk, her later vocal production of a CD about her journey's highlights and the growing popularity of her mentoring sessions on radio, TV and at lectures, proved that her manuscript was a publication begging to be published with White Knight's social issues.

Sue Kenney's My Camino became the end result of our many intense sessions as I grew to understand the quality of this author's soul mission to the rapidly-changing world that I saw as becoming so in need of her message.

White Knight's concern for publishing books filled with social issues is well book-marked by Sue Kenney's story.

V. Wm. (Bill) Belfontaine)

White Knight's Remarkable Women series

In keeping with White Knight Publication's mandate to bring great titles of social concern to book and library shelves across North America, I am indeed fortunate as publisher to have been closely involved with the latest publications in White Knight's "Remarkable Women Series" listed below.

Conscious Women — Conscious Lives

A unique book that lives up to expectations that women across North America constantly provide the nurturing component that continues to make our countries so great. These stories from across Canada and the United States of America, bring home those concerns that women have for other women providing love, nourishment and hope for our present and future generations. Remarkable women, everyone.
ISBN 0-9734186-1-3   216 pages
PB US $13.95 Cdn $19.95

Sharing MS

This informative book by the author and two women friends with Multiple Sclerosis, is a beacon of common sense lighting the way of those who have MS or suspect they may be afflicted, as well as being helpful to family, friends and health professionals. Read the book then call the MS Society Chapter in your local telephone book for information about your concerns regarding Multiple Sclerosis.
ISBN 0-9730949-7-4   218 pages
PB US $13.95 Cdn $19.95

The Unusual Life and Times of Nancy Ford-Inman

This story is about a most remarkable woman who contributed so much to Britain's literature, the theatre, media and the war effort in spite of a major physical handicap. Badly crippled by Cerebral Palsy at an early age yet she fought her way to become the author of almost 60 romantic novels and journalistic endeavors too numerous to count.
ISBN 0-9730949-8-2   238 pages
PB US $13.95 Cdn $19.95

Genres of White Knight Publications

Biography
The Life and Times of
Nancy Ford-Inman
– Nancy Erb Kee

Gay Adoption
A Swim Against The Tide
– David R.I. McKinstry

Inspiration – Self Help
Conscious Women –
Conscious Lives
– Darlene Montgomery
Sharing MS (Multiple Sclerosis)
– Linda Ironside
Sue Kenney's My Camino
– Sue Kenney

Personal Finances
Don't Borrow Money Until You
Read This Book
– Paul Counter

Poetry
Two Voices – A Circle of Love
– Serena Williamson Andrew

Politics
Turning Points – Ray Argyle

Self-help
Books by Dr. K. Sohail
• *Love, Sex and Marriage*
• *The Art of Living in Your*
   Green Zone
• *The Art of Loving in Your*
   Green Zone
• *The Art of Working in Your*
   Green Zone

True Crime – Police
10-45 Says Death
– Kathy McCormack Carter
Life on Homicide,
– Former Toronto Police Chief
Bill McCormack
The Myth of The Chosen One
– Dr. K. Sohail

Recommended reading from
other publishers
HISTORY
An Amicable Friendship
– Jan Th. J. Krijff
RELIGION
From Islam to Secular
   Humanism – Dr. K. Sohail
Gabriel's Dragon
   – Arch Priest Fr. Antony
   Gabriel
Pro Deo
   – Prof Ronald M Smith

READING LIST AND WEB SITES

...ccitti, Barbara. *Pate, Jam & Good Intentions*,
..arbara Cappuccitti. Toronto.

...ho, Paulo. *The Pilgrimage*, Perennial, An Imprint of Harper
..Collins, New York. ISBN 0-06-251279-X

..nfraternity of St James, *Camino Frances Pilgrim Guides to Spain*,
..Confraternity of St James, London. ISBN 1-870585-57-7

..ennett, Laurie. *A hug for the apostle*, MacMillan of Canada.
..Toronto. ISBN 0-771-5919-0

..Elyn, Aviva. *Following the Milky Way*, Pilgrim's Process Inc.
..ISBN 0-9710609-0

Frey, Nancy Louise. *Pilgrim Stories*, University of California Press.
..ISBN 0-520-25754-9

Gitlitz, David M., and DAVIDSON, Linda Kay. *The pilgrim road to Santiago: the complete cultural handbook*. St Martin's Griffin, New York. ISBN 0-312-25416-4

Lambert, Craig. *Mind Over Water*, Houghton Mifflin Company, New York. ISBN 0-395-85716-3

MacLaine, Shirley. *The Camino A Journey of the Spirit*, Pocket Books. New York. ISBN 0-7434-0073-9

Melczer, William. *The Pilgrim's Guide to Santiago de Compostela*, Italica Press, New York. ISBN 0934977-25-9

Roddis, Miles; Frey, Nancy; Placer, Jose; Fletcher, Mathew; Noble, John; *Lonely Planet, Walking in Spain*, Victoria, Lonely Planet Publications Pty Ltd. ISBN 0-86442-543-0

Ward, Robert. *Virgin Trails, A Secular Pilgrimage*, Key Porter Books, Toronto. ISBN 1-55263-374-8

York, Sarah. *Pilgrim Heart, The Inner Journey Home*, Jossey-Bass, San Francisco. ISBN 0-7879-5695-3

Web Sites   www.santiago.ca
     www.ultreya.net
     www.santiagobis.com
     www.csj.org.uk
     gocamino@pete.uri.edu